GREAT MOMENTS IN BASEBALL

A CENTURY OF BASEBALL'S FINEST

PUBLICATIONS INTERNATIONAL, LTD.

Louis Weber, C.E.O.
Publications International, Ltd.
7373 North Cicero Avenue
Lincolnwood, Illinois 60646

Printed and bound in Yugoslavia.

8 7 6 5 4 3 2 1

ISBN 0-88176-913-4

Library of Congress Catalog Card Number
90-83418

CONTENTS

CONTENTS

THE CENTURY'S TRIUMPHS OF BASEBALL

This publication, *Great Moments in Baseball,* covers all of the exceptional highlights and significant events, and the players who accomplished them, from 1901 to the present. With interesting profiles, hundreds of photographs, and numerous essays, this book captures the outstanding feats that help define America's pastime.

Eighty of the century's exceptional moments are presented in chronological order, from Nap Lajoie's Triple Crown season in 1901 that helped establish the American League as a legitimate major league to ageless Nolan Ryan's record sixth no-hitter in 1990. Included are hundreds of evocative photographs, many in full color. Feel the excitement as you witness Carlton Fisk's homer in the 1975 World Series and Cookie Lavagetto's double in 1947's fall classic. Essays are included that describe other events or players to illuminate the specific moment or the time in baseball.

The World Series set the stage for many memorable occurrences. Babe Ruth's legendary "called shot" in the 1932 Series may or may not have happened, but the fable surely enhanced the legend surrounding the career of the Bambino. In 1954, Willie Mays caught a Vic Wertz line drive at full speed for what many think is the finest defensive play of all time. It is now simply known as "The Catch." For one day—October 8, 1956—Yankee Don Larsen was the best pitcher to ever step on the rubber in World Series history as he threw a perfect game.

Individual players become frozen in time because of outstanding performances. Bobby Thomson's "shot heard 'round the world" in 1951 helped bring baseball into the television era. Roger Maris's enormous single-season record 61st home run in 1961 made him one of history's most-recognized players. And Sandy Amoros in 1955 helped the Brooklyn Dodgers finally beat the Yankees by making a miracle catch to rob Yogi Berra of a run-scoring double.

Some of the most memorable feats in the history of baseball include the unlikely teams that became champions. In 1950, the Philadelphia Phillies "Whiz Kids" came out of nowhere to win the NL pennant behind their great pitching staff of Jim Konstanty and Robin Roberts. The 1969 Miracle Mets were led by pitcher Tom Seaver and manager Gil Hodges to a World Championship.

From 1901 to the present, the interesting profiles, the hundreds of photographs, and the numerous essays in *Great Moments in Baseball* capture the best that the sport has to offer.

NAP LAJOIE WINS TRIPLE CROWN IN AL's FIRST YEAR

The American League opened for business as a second major league in 1901 and raided National League rosters for established "name" players. It was a young star, however, who did the most to validate the credibility of the new league.

Napoleon "Nap" Lajoie was a slick-fielding 26-year-old second baseman who had batted .326, .361, .324, .378, and .337 in his first five seasons for the Philadelphia Phillies (very good, but not unthinkable batting averages for the high-scoring late 1890s). His career, however, had given little hint of what was to come. Playing for the Athletics in 1901, the Phillies' cross-town American League competitors, Lajoie put on a one-man slugging exhibition and won the century's first Triple Crown. He led the AL in hitting at .426, in home runs with 14, and in RBI with 125.

This Triple Crown is retrospective, since the concept did not exist in 1901; triples, not home runs, were the power stat of the day, and the RBI did not become official until 1920. But in 1901 there was no shortage of important offensive categories dominated by Lajoie. He led the new league in runs with 145, hits with 232, doubles with 48, on-base average at .451, and slugging percentage at .643. His .426 batting average is the highest mark of this century. Besides Lajoie, only Rogers Hornsby in the 20th century has won the Triple Crown with a batting average over .400. While some say that Lajoie's 1901 numbers were inflated because AL competition was still a cut below NL standards and because foul balls were not counted as strikes in 1901, it must be remembered that all of this was no less true for Lajoie than for all of the men he outhit.

Lajoie could not single-handedly win the pennant; the A's pitching let them down, and they finished fourth. But Phillies' fans followed him to the new league in droves. He helped plant a secure AL foothold in one of the three key markets (the others were Chicago and Boston) in which the AL had chosen to take on National League teams on their own turf. Lajoie's contract status then became the main battleground in the war between the leagues when the Phillies sued to get him back and obtained an injunction from the state courts that forbade Lajoie from playing for any team but the Phillies in 1902. A's manager Connie Mack, knowing how important Lajoie's drawing power was to the AL's survival, hit upon the ingenious dodge of sending Lajoie to play for AL Cleveland, where he would be outside the Pennsylvania court's jurisdiction. There, with the exception of away games in Philadelphia, he played out the 1902 season, batting .378.

After the two leagues made peace in 1903, Lajoie remained with Cleveland for 12 years and won three more batting titles.

Nap Lajoie was one of the best second basemen of all time. A big man (about 195 lbs.), he hit 648 doubles in his career. He was a manager of the Cleveland American League team (named the Naps in his honor) from 1905 to 1909. Lajoie relinquished his managerial role because he felt it diminished his play between the lines and thus hurt the team.

Ban Johnson

American League's first season

From its founding in 1876 until the turn of the century, the National League faced repeated challenges from upstart leagues. Only one succeeded—the American League.

The man behind the AL, formerly the minor Western League, was Commissioner Ban Johnson. He insisted on a clean brand of play, free from the rowdiness and umpire-baiting that were the norm in the NL.

In 1901, the American League debuted in Chicago, Boston, Detroit, Philadelphia, Baltimore, Washington, Cleveland, and Milwaukee. The fans responded to the AL's style, as well as to the many stars—such as John McGraw, Cy Young, and Jimmy Collins—that it had lured from the NL with higher salaries. The two leagues made peace in 1903, giving baseball 50 years of stability and prosperity.

AL BOSTON WINS FIRST MODERN WORLD SERIES

Jimmy Collins, player/manager of the 1903 Boston Pilgrims.

The 1903 season began on a note of goodwill, with the NL and the AL agreeing to coexist. During the season, two of the more sporting owners, Barney Dreyfus of Pittsburgh and Henry Killilea of Boston, whose teams were running away with their leagues' pennants, agreed to play a best five-of-nine postseason series. This competition was fierce, unlike the meaningless Temple Cup series of the 1890s.

The AL's Boston Pilgrims seemed to be overmatched against one of the greatest dynasties in NL history. Pittsburgh won its third straight pennant in 1903, with player/manager Fred Clarke; hitting stars Honus Wagner, Ginger Beaumont, and Tommy Leach; and a brilliant pitching staff of Deacon Phillippe, Sam Leever, and Ed Doheny. In 1902 Clarke's wrecking crew had taken the flag by 27$\frac{1}{2}$ games in a 142-game schedule. Pittsburgh was 91-49 in 1903, winning the pennant by six and one-half games.

The 16,242 Pilgrim fans who filled Boston's Huntington Avenue Grounds for game one hung their hopes on a number of late-season injuries to key Pirates; Leever had hurt his shoulder, Doheny had suffered a mental breakdown and was hospitalized, and the great Wagner had a bad leg. Nevertheless the visitors beat Cy Young 7-3, as Leach's two triples and Jimmy Sebring's home run picked up the slack and Phillippe struck out 10 and walked none on a six-hitter. After Boston evened matters behind Big Bill Dinneen in game two, Phillippe returned on a day's rest to win again in game three, 4-2. Incredibly, Clarke started Phillippe again in game four, played in Pittsburgh only three days later on October 6. Though his arm was showing signs of strain (he struck out only one in nine innings), he won again, beating Dinneen 5-4. The Series now stood at Boston one game, Phillippe three.

The tide turned in games five and six, when Young shut down the Pirates 11-2 and Dinneen won 6-3. The two Boston pitchers then took complete control of the rest of the Series as their team won four straight to become World Champions, five games to three. Young and Dinneen allowed the opposition a total of five earned runs in the final four contests and twice defeated an exhausted Phillippe, who received little support from his teammates either in the field or at bat.

In 1904, John McGraw of the NL-pennant-winning New York Giants, who held a grudge from his unhappy stay in the American League, refused to meet the AL pennant winner. He also thought that the New York Highlanders might win the AL pennant, and he didn't want to risk the Giants losing the Series and thus the team's top ranking among the New York fans. But in 1905 the two leagues decreed that the World Series be made permanent.

Deacon Phillippe (top) didn't reach the majors until age 27, but he won 186 games. He gave up only nine walks in 1910, his last full season. The 1903 Pirates (bottom), winners of a third straight National League pennant. Fred Clark is third from the left in the front row; Honus Wagner is at the far left of the middle row.

Deacon Phillippe's five World Series complete games

The peak of Deacon Phillippe's career, his 25-9, 2.43 ERA season in 1903, was topped by an amazing postseason. He started five of the eight World Series games, winning three and completing all five. Phillippe pitched 44 innings over 13 days—obviously not a record that was made to be broken. He gave up only three walks and had 22 strikeouts, allowing 14 earned runs for a 2.86 ERA.

Phillippe won 20 five years in a row from 1899 to 1903. He was certainly the greatest control artist of his day. Phillippe allowed 1.5 bases on balls or less per nine innings in 10 of his 11 full seasons, and he finished his career with only 363 walks in 2,608 innings.

JACK CHESBRO'S WILD PITCH BLOWS PENNANT

Pitcher Jack Chesbro is remembered today for setting the modern record for wins in a season with 41. In his own time, however, Chesbro was famous for a very different exploit—a wild pitch that lost an American League pennant for the New York Highlanders. Strangely enough, he performed both of these feats in the same year, 1904.

Boston and New York took turns in first place down the stretch of the 1904 pennant race. The two clubs had little else in common. Under Hall-of-Famer Jimmy Collins, Boston fielded the same star-filled lineup that had won the 1903 flag by 14½ games. Clark Griffith's Highlanders finished dead last in Baltimore in 1902 before moving to New York in 1903. With a patchwork of no-name rookies and such older players as Wee Willie Keeler and Griffith himself, New York's 1904 squad resembled an expansion team more than a dynasty.

The greatest difference between the teams was pitching. Boston had a solid four-man rotation. The thin Highlander staff became a two-man show of Chesbro and Jack Powell, who started 96 games between them and completed 86. Chesbro led the AL in innings with 455, games with 55, and complete games with 48. On that final day against Boston, Griffith gave Chesbro the ball one more time.

Boston brought a slim one and one-half game lead into New York for two final games on Monday, October 10. With no tie possible, it was doubleheader sweep or nothing for the Highlanders; the 15,000-seat Hilltop Park was filled beyond capacity.

Chesbro dueled Boston pitcher Bill Dinneen until the fifth inning, when New York scored twice; two innings later, Boston tied it up when second baseman Jimmy Williams threw away Dinneen's easy grounder with runners on second and third.

It was still 2-2 in the Boston ninth when a single, a sacrifice, and an infield out moved a man to third with shortstop Freddy Parent at bat. With the count at 1-2, Chesbro let fly with his out-pitch, a hard-sinking spitball. But the pitch eluded the catcher, young Red Kleinow, and Boston won the game and the pennant, 3-2. New York won what must have been a very dreary second game, 1-0 in 10 innings.

Many contemporary authorities thought that Kleinow should have handled the pitch and that Chesbro's selection as the goat was unfair. Even after Chesbro's death in 1931, Chesbro's wife and others campaigned to have the scorer's decision changed from wild pitch to passed ball. Regardless, there are other points in Chesbro's defense: The Highlanders still had the bottom of the ninth to come back, there was Williams's key error, and New York still had to win the second game.

Chesbro's good name seems to have been restored simply because his 41-12 season is still in the record books.

Even after Jack Chesbro's death in 1931, his wife continued her efforts to have his famous wild pitch officially changed to a passed ball. Rookie receiver Red Kleinow, and not the dependable Deacon McGuire, was behind the plate when Chesbro made his ill-fated pitch.

CHRISTY MATHEWSON HURLS THREE SERIES SHUTOUTS

It was a pitchers' year in the AL. American League hitters batted a combined .241 in 1905, and the pennant-winning Athletics led the league with a .255 batting average and only 623 runs scored. After a tough pennant race in which Philadelphia barely survived a late-season surge by Chicago—which compiled a 1.99 team ERA—Connie Mack's A's were looking forward to facing the New York Giants pitching in the World Series.

The pre-Series wisdom rated the New York pitching staff, with Christy Mathewson (31-8, 1.27 ERA) and Joe McGinnity (21-15, 2.87 ERA), about even with the Philly rotation—including Rube Waddell (27-10, 1.48 ERA), Eddie Plank (24-12, 2.26 ERA), and Chief Bender (18-11, 2.83 ERA). But that was before the eccentric Waddell hurt his shoulder while playfully wrestling with a teammate and put himself out of action. As it turned out, John McGraw and his Giants embarrassed Philadelphia four games to one. The New York pitchers so dominated the Series that the only difference a healthy Waddell would have made is if he notched a few hits.

Mathewson, a 26-year-old righty with a mystifying screwball, was in top form in game one and beat Plank 3-0, allowing four hits and no walks in nine innings. He also stopped the most direct scoring threat he faced in the Series by fielding a bunt and throwing out a baserunner at home. Bender evened the Series with a shutout of his own, winning 3-0 over McGinnity. The roof then fell in on the A's. Matty threw another four-hitter to win game three 9-0. He walked one batter, but no Athletic got past first base. McGinnity won game four 1-0 on third baseman Lave Cross's error in the fourth inning. Mathewson clinched the Series by scattering six hits and defeating Bender 2-0. Matty retired the last 10 batters that he faced in the Series.

Besides setting a still-unchallenged record by pitching three shutouts in a single Series, Mathewson allowed 14 hits and just one walk in 27 innings; he struck out 18. While he was on the mound, not a single Athletics runner reached third. And Mathewson did this all in six days.

The Series composite score, 15-3, which could be mistaken for the score of one game, underlines the irony that 1905 was one of the best-pitched World Series of all time—and yet it was one of the most lopsided. The A's hit no triples and no home runs; they had 23 more strikeouts than RBI. Six Philadelphia regulars batted under .200. Adding in McGinnity's 17 innings of work and Ames's one, the New York pitchers allowed the A's a grand total of 25 hits and five walks in 45 innings.

Years later, McGraw would say that of all his great teams, this team came nearest to perfection. Certainly none improved on the 1905 Giants' Series ERA—0.00.

Christy Mathewson was considered by most observers to have been the best pitcher in the game during the first decade of the century. Many baseball historians feel that he was the best righthander ever.

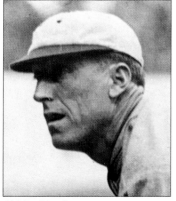

Eddie Plank

Each of five games in 1905 Series is shutout

Four World Series in the 86-year history of the Fall Classic—1920, 1956, 1958, and 1966—have had as many as three shutouts. Five shutouts in five games seems almost unthinkable.

The 1905 Series was the meeting point for four pitchers whose names are now enshrined in Cooperstown: Christy Mathewson, Joe McGinnity, Eddie Plank, and Chief Bender. In 1905 baseball fans saw a World Series in which 78 out of 88, or 89 percent, of the total innings were pitched by Hall of Famers. A total of six pitchers (from both teams) tallied 88 innings for six complete games. They allowed 56 hits, seven earned runs, 20 bases on balls, and 51 strikeouts.

CUBS WIN 116 GAMES BUT LOSE SERIES TO WHITE SOX

Frank Chance guided the Cubs to four flags in five years.

No league in history has ever been as dominated by a team as was the 1906 National League by Frank Chance's incipient Chicago Cub dynasty. His team won 116 games, still a record, and lost only 36. A 50-7 stretch drive that included a 26-3 run in August expanded the Cubs' margin over second-place New York to 20 games and 66½ games over last-place Boston. Led by Three Finger Brown's nine shutouts, the Chicago pitchers racked up an incredible 30. The experts made the Cubs heavily favored in the World Series against the cross-town Chicago White Sox, who were a mere 93-58 on the season.

The experts should have known better. The Sox, nicknamed "The Hitless Wonders," may have scored 135 fewer runs than did the Cubs, but they were very good at the four dead-ball fundamentals: pitching, fielding, basestealing, and the ability to get on base. Behind Big Ed Walsh, who threw 10 shutouts and had an ERA of 1.88; Doc White, whose 1.52 ERA led the league; and Nick Altrock (2.06 ERA) and Frank Owen (22 wins); the Sox were far from outclassed by the Cubs staff of Brown, Ed Reulbach, Orval Overall, and Jack Pfiester, each under 2.00 in ERA. While the Cubs had sluggers like Wildfire Shulte (13 triples) and Harry Steinfeldt (league-leading 83 RBI), the White Sox countered with Fielder Jones and Ed Hahn (second and third in the AL in walks), and Frank Isbell (third in stolen bases).

Sure enough, tough pitching—aided by cold weather and snow flurries—was the theme of the Series' first four games. The Sox took game one 2-1 behind Altrock, and won game three 3-0 when a sixth-inning, bases-loaded triple by third baseman George Rohe supported Walsh's 12-strike-out, two-hit masterpiece. The Cubs won games two and four, both contests featuring dramatic no-hit bids carried into the late innings by Reulbach and Brown. True to their nickname, the White Sox had scored only six runs on 11 hits through game four, yet they were tied in the Series 2-2.

Sunshine and higher temperatures pushed attendance over 20,000 for the first time in the Series in game five; both teams' bats warmed up as well. The White Sox knocked out Reulbach in the second inning and Pfiester in the fourth; Walsh was shaky but survived to win 8-6. In the deciding game, Doc White's seven-hit, four-walk effort was good enough to beat the Cubs 8-3, as a tired Brown put his team in the hole by allowing seven earned runs in one and two-thirds innings.

The MVPs of the 1906 World Series were the members of the White Sox pitching staff, whose 1.50 ERA performance upset a Cubs dynasty that would go on to win four pennants and average 106 wins a season between 1906 and 1910.

An action shot from the 1906 World Series (top), the first to pit two teams from the same city against each other and the only one to feature two Chicago clubs. Doc White (bottom), later a dentist, gave the White Sox 160 wins after jumping from the Phillies to the American League after the 1902 season.

White Sox pitcher Ed Walsh

White Sox win 19 in a row during 1906 season

They may not have won 116 games, but the White Sox won 19 straight games, the longest streak in American League history.

The Sox needed every one of them. When the streak began on August 2, they were nine games out in fourth place; eleven days later they were in first by a half-game. For an encore they swept three in Boston and four against second-place New York.

Perhaps the least likely team in history to put together a winning streak—with an ERA of 2.13 and a batting average of .230—they played a tremendous number of tight, low-scoring games. Nothing came easy for the Sox. They barely nosed out New York at the wire.

THE TRIBUNE ALWAYS MAKES A HIT WITH ITS SPORTING

'MERKLE BLUNDER' ULTIMATELY LOSES PENNANT FOR GIANTS

Fred Merkle

Fans in 1908 saw two of the most exciting pennant races ever. Three NL teams finished within one game of first; Detroit won a four-team AL race by .004, the smallest margin of victory in history. However, both were overshadowed by the "Merkle Blunder."

Fred Merkle was a competent first baseman who hit .273 over a 16-year career. But during that time, Giants fans never stopped calling him "Bonehead" and saying "So long, Fred. Don't forget to touch second." Merkle took the heckling so hard that years later he admitted it was tough for him to play.

On September 23, Merkle was a substitute in a game against the Cubs, who trailed New York in the standings by .006. With two out in the bottom of the ninth inning in a 1-1 game, Merkle singled Moose McCormick over to third. Al Bridwell then singled to center, McCormick scored the winning run, and Merkle made for the Giants' clubhouse to avoid the crowd, which was spilling onto the infield. He didn't bother to touch second. Today, thanks to Merkle, every player makes sure to touch second under these circumstances; otherwise the defense can tag the base for the force-out and nullify the run.

According to the Cubs, this is just what happened. Second baseman Johnny Evers somehow, in the midst of the confusion, retrieved the ball and tagged second in view of plate umpire Hank O'Day, who told base umpire Robert Emslie to call the absent Merkle out. With resumption impossible, O'Day ruled the game a tie and ignited a firestorm of protests and counterprotests. Some witnesses said they saw Merkle touch the base. Others claimed that Evers's ball was not the game ball.

Significantly, Evers had had a run-in with O'Day in an identical situation in a game against Pittsburgh two weeks earlier. There O'Day had declared that the run counted, but was stung when Chicago protested officially to league President Harry Pulliam. Though O'Day's call was upheld, it is doubtless that the protest intimidated O'Day. One thing is sure—Merkle's play was a blunder only in retrospect. Merkle could never have suspected that O'Day would call him out on a never-before-enforced technicality, that his team would finish tied with Chicago, that Pulliam would order a postseason replay, or that the Giants would lose the makeup game and the pennant.

The Merkle affair was painful all around. O'Day was reviled by colleague Bill Klem, who called it "the worst call in the history of baseball." Fans and the press debated the matter all winter. Many thought Giants manager John McGraw should have known about the Pittsburgh incident and cautioned his players. Eventually, baseball seems to have agreed to scapegoat Merkle and leave it at that.

Even today, many followers of the game know Fred Merkle's name, but few know that the Giants first baseman had an otherwise excellent 16-year career and played in five World Series.

Umpire Hank O'Day's great career

With baseball under the influence of disciplinarian Ban Johnson, umpires in the 1900s enjoyed respect, not to mention safety, unheard of in the rowdy 1880s and 1890s. The new generation of umpires, men like Bill Klem, were dignified and professional.

Hank O'Day was from the old school. A hard-bitten former major league pitcher and, according to writer Hugh Fullerton, a notorious "bullhead," O'Day prided himself on never being a "homer." He carried the scars to prove it—mementos of a day at the St. Louis ballpark in the 1890s when he was severely beaten by an angry mob and had to be rescued by the police. O'Day umpired for 35 years in the NL.

WAGNER'S PIRATES BEAT COBB'S TIGERS IN SERIES

Of all the hitters in the low-scoring 1900s, Honus Wagner in the NL and Ty Cobb in the AL were the most celebrated. But fans had to wait until 1909 to see them play each other in a World Series.

A 10-time batting champion, Cobb regularly led the AL in hits, runs, and stolen bases. He drove his heavy-hitting Tigers to their third straight pennant in 1909, leading the league in batting average (.377), slugging average (.517), on-base average (.431), and nearly every other category. A virtuoso performance like this needed only a supporting cast, which was ably provided by slugging Sam Crawford and an above-average pitching staff.

Wagner was just as dominating in the NL. Easily the greatest shortstop who ever lived, he won eight batting titles and drove in or scored 100 runs in a season 15 times, an incredible figure for dead-ball days. The Pirates were a more balanced team than the Tigers, with first-class pitching including Howie Camnitz and Vic Willis, along with Babe Adams, who went 12-3 as a spot starter with the lowest ERA of any rookie in history, 1.11. Tommy Leach and Fred Clarke augmented a versatile attack. Wagner matched Cobb by leading the NL in batting average (.339), slugging percentage (.489), and on-base average (.420).

Unfortunately, the Cobb versus Wagner face-off flopped. Cobb stole home in Detroit's 7-2 victory in game two, but managed only a .231 average for the seven-game Series. Wagner batted .333 and outstole Cobb six bases to two.

The undisputed star of the Series, however, was young Babe Adams. The frenzied Pirates fans who filled monumental new Forbes Field saw Adams—player/manager Clarke's surprise pick to start the opener— handle the Tigers easily and win on a six-hitter, 4-1. The two teams traded wins until game five, when Adams survived a pair of home runs to outduel Ed Summers 8-4. After Detroit came back in game six, Clarke bet everything on Adams in the seventh game. He had saved his best for last; while Wild Bill Donovan lived up to his nickname by walking six in three innings, Adams coolly threw a six-hit shutout to clinch the Series for Pittsburgh and bring his Series record to 3-0. His amazing command of his slow breaking pitches had frustrated the entire Tigers lineup—but above all Cobb, who was held to a single hit in 11 at-bats.

Though they played a combined 27 more years in the majors, neither Cobb nor Wagner would get another chance to improve his disappointing —.262 and .275 respectively—career postseason batting average. Adams, however, was still around when the Pirates won their next pennant in 1925; at the age of 43 he pitched one scoreless inning to lower his World Series ERA to 1.29, the ninth-best of all time.

Pittsburgh Pirates shortstop Honus Wagner (left) *and Detroit Tigers outfielder Ty Cobb compare bats during the 1909 World Series. The two greatest players of their day faced each other only on that one occasion.*

Ty Cobb

They may have been well-matched on the field, but in character Ty Cobb couldn't have been more different from the gentle Honus Wagner.

Cobb's almost psychotic aggression has achieved mythic proportions through the well-known tales of his fearless baserunning and his many off-field run-ins with teammates and fans; yet most of the stories are true. Fortunately for society, Cobb channeled most of his fury into baseball—he is still first all-time in career batting average and runs scored, and second in hits—and into the stock market, where his early investments in General Motors and Coca-Cola made him baseball's first player-millionaire.

HOME RUN BAKER SLAMS TWO IN SERIES

Frank "Home Run" Baker

His stats, by modern standards, indicate that Home Run Baker was no power-hitter. Baker hit 96 home runs in 13 years and never more than 12 in a season. Two things that are not so well known about Baker are: 1) In his day, Baker was a premier home run hitter, having led the AL for four straight years from 1911 to '14 with totals of 11, 10, 12, and 9, and 2) that this feat has nothing to do with his nickname. For most of his career the third baseman for the powerhouse 1910s Philadelphia Athletics, Frank Baker was called "Home Run" because of two clutch homers that he hit during the 1911 World Series.

The Giants overthrew Chicago in 1911 on the strength of pitching aces Rube Marquard and Christy Mathewson. The A's and their "$100,000 Infield"—Baker at third base, Jack Barry at shortstop, Eddie Collins at second base, and Stuffy McInnis at first base—were run-away winners over Detroit in their race. The 1911 World Series thus became a rematch of the 1905 encounter. It started almost the same way, with Mathewson winning 2-1 on a six-hitter. Game two was another close affair as Eddie Plank and Marquard allowed only nine hits and no walks between them. The score was 1-1 in the sixth inning when Marquard, who had retired the last 13 A's, allowed a two-out double to Eddie Collins and then a home run that Baker pulled over the short right field wall. Philadelphia won, 3-1.

Many of the stars on both sides of the '11 Series were putting their names to ghost-written "inside" accounts of the games in daily newspapers; Mathewson's game two story criticized Marquard for leaving the fatal pitch up and out over the plate in Baker's hitting zone, instead of inside where Giants manager John McGraw had told him to pitch it. Then, for eight and one-third innings in game three, Mathewson nursed a 1-0 lead over A's pitcher Jack Coombs when Baker came up to the plate. This time Baker swatted an inside pitch into the right field stands, tying the score; the A's went on to win 3-2 on an 11th-inning rally that featured a key single by Baker. In his ghost-written piece the next morning, Marquard let Mathewson know what he thought of his pitching advice.

Now known from coast to coast as "Home Run," Baker had hit his last home run in the Series but wasn't through punishing the Giants pitching staff. Baker walked and doubled twice to beat Matty 4-2 in game four (which was delayed six days by rain). Baker collected two more hits in game six, as Chief Bender wrapped it up for Philadelphia, 13-2. All told, Baker had nine hits in 24 at-bats for a Series-high .375 average; he also led all hitters with seven runs, five RBI, and two out of the three home runs hit by both teams combined.

Home Run Baker (top) *led the American League in homers four years in a row despite never hitting more than 12 in a season. The $100,000 Infield* (bottom). *By the end of the 1915 season only Stuffy McInnis* (far left) *remained with the A's after the four began demanding that Connie Mack pay them their worth.*

SNODGRASS'S MUFF
JINXES GIANTS' BID

The National League was under a postseason jinx throughout the 1910s, losing eight out of 10 World Series. This was never more apparent than in the exciting, strange, and—for seven games and nine innings—well-played 1912 edition. John McGraw's New York Giants won 103 games, leading the NL in runs scored and ERA. In the World Series, the Giants outhit the Boston Red Sox .270 to .220 and allowed a full earned run less per game. Yet somehow they managed to lose, 4-3.

In game one, McGraw sacrificed rookie spitballer Jeff Tesreau to Smokey Joe Wood, who was coming off an overpowering 34-5 season, losing 6-4. The tactic misfired when Christy Mathewson was wasted in a second-game 6-6 tie that was halted by darkness. Giant pitcher Rube Marquard won game three 2-1 and Wood beat Tesreau again. Young Hugh Bedient won over Matty in another 2-1 game, and Marquard won his second game 5-2 in game six. Wood pitched against Tesreau in game seven but was unexpectedly shelled by the Giants, who won 11-4 to force an eighth-game showdown between Mathewson and Bedient.

For nine innings both teams threatened in nearly every turn at bat, banging out a combined total of 14 hits, but could only push across two runs. In the fifth, Boston's Harry Hooper made a game-saving play when he leapt into the stands and brought back a Larry Doyle home run *barehanded.* Mathewson and Wood, who had come in after the seventh, walked a 1-1 tightrope into extra innings. Then in the Giants half of the tenth, slugging outfielder Red Murray doubled and Fred Merkle singled him home. Now it was New York's turn to feel confident, with the great Mathewson needing to go just one more inning to clinch the Series.

In that inning, though, normally steady Giants center fielder Fred Snodgrass dropped an easy fly ball to put leadoff batter Clyde Engel on second. Hooper later said that mistake "could have happened to anybody" but has been immortalized as the "$30,000 Muff" (after the Series winners' share). Snodgrass made a great catch on the next batter that erased a certain extra-base hit, but when the time came to choose a goat for the Giants' 3-2 defeat, this play was forgotten and Snodgrass was the unanimous choice.

There were other candidates for the honor. Mathewson got Tris Speaker to pop up in foul territory near first base, but Matty confused first baseman Merkle and catcher Chief Meyers by calling for Meyers—who was farther from the play—to take it. Neither made the catch. Speaker then singled the tying run home and the go-ahead run to third; Larry Gardner won the Series with a sacrifice fly that should have been the third out.

Fred Snodgrass lived to be 86 years old but could not outlive his famous 1912 World Series muff; it was headlined in many of his obituary notices. Nicknamed "Snow," Snodgrass played in three fall classics for the New York Giants.

WALTER JOHNSON EARNS PITCHING TRIPLE CROWN

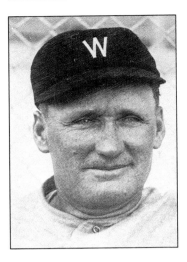

In spite of all its emphasis on individual heroics, baseball remains a team sport. Nothing illustrates this better than Walter Johnson's 1913 season. The greatest righthander who ever lived, "The Big Train" threw his whiplike sidearm fastball (and not much else) for two decades. He won 416 games—110 by shutouts—while losing only 279, and his all-time record of 3,508 strikeouts stood for half a century. Yet Johnson's team, the Washington Senators, was a loser for nearly all of his career. Washington finished seventh or eighth five times in five years between 1907 and 1911. Even The Big Train's peak performances during the early 1910s propelled the Senators no higher in the standings than second.

Spotted out West by a traveling cigar salesman, who sent awed descriptions of the 19-year-old bush leaguer's mighty fastball ("he knows where it's going, otherwise there'd be dead bodies all over Idaho") to the Senators, Johnson arrived in the big leagues in 1907 as green as could be. After conquering early wildness (he threw 21 wild pitches in 1910), he hit his stride in 1912, going 33-12 and striking out 303 to help Washington move up five places in the standings to second.

The following year, Johnson topped this with the best performance of his career and one of the greatest pitching seasons in history, when he went 36-7 and led the 1913 AL in wins, ERA (1.14), and strikeouts (243) to become one of only six American League pitchers ever to win the "pitching triple crown." His 1.14 ERA, the fourth-lowest of all time, combined with his league-best 11 shutouts and 55$\frac{2}{3}$ consecutive scoreless innings (a record that stood until 1968) demonstrate Johnson's utter dominance of AL hitters.

After the blazing fastball, The Big Train's biggest weapon was control. Though his strikeout total dropped by 60 from the previous year, he cut his walks in half to 38 and wild pitches down to three. His opponents batted only .187 against him and had an on-base percentage of .217; the league batting average was .256 and on-base percentage was .325. Still, even with their number-one pitcher 29 games over .500, the Senators won only 90 games and finished six and one-half games behind Philadelphia. The drop-off in talent from Johnson to the rest of the 1913 Senators is shown by the shocking differential in their winning percentages; Johnson at .837 and the rest of the team 351 points lower at .486.

His greatest season more or less told the story of the rest of Johnson's career, which lasted until 1927. Though he won 20 or more games for the next six years, Washington settled back into the second division. It wasn't until 1924 that the Senators won the pennant. They then beat the Giants in the World Series 4-3, with Johnson winning game seven in relief.

Walter Johnson's 416 wins and 3,508 strikeouts are only part of the story; in 1925, he set a record for pitchers when he rapped .433 with 42 hits. Johnson and fellow Washington pitcher Joe Boehling had a combined 53-14 record in 1913, while the rest of the Senators staff was a dreary 37-50.

MIRACLE BRAVES MARCH TO CHAMPIONSHIP

Pitcher Bill James won 26 games for the 1914 Braves.

According to the sports pages and barroom conversations, to win a pennant you need only hustle, clutch hitting, and defense. The 1914 "Miracle Braves" came from last place to prove that point.

The story of the underdog Boston Braves' journey from last place in July to the pennant begins and ends the same way: with a fit of pique. Disappointed in his team's third-place finish in 1913, Cubs' owner Charles Murphy traded star second baseman Johnny Evers to the Braves. Evers became, along with hard-fighting shortstop Rabbit Maranville, the heart of the Boston club. Evers was voted the NL's MVP for 1914, beating out his double-play partner by six votes. Evers led the team with 81 runs and a .390 on-base average. He led the league second basemen in fielding, and he and Maranville led in double plays. Boston had a scrappy, opportunistic offense, one of the best defensive teams ever, and an innovative manager in George Stallings.

Stallings was a great motivator and an early practitioner of platooning. Boston had very good pitching, led by Bill James and Dick Rudolph, but no sluggers to speak of. Maranville set an NL record for putouts and the major league record for total chances at shortstop, and he had a team-high 78 RBI with a .246 average and only 33 extra-base hits.

With Maranville out sick, the 1914 Braves won only four of their first 22. By mid-June they were still in last place, but the front-running New York Giants had been unable to move away from the pack. The Braves then began a dizzying 34-10 pennant drive with eight straight wins. On July 21 the Braves moved into fourth. Another winning streak, this time nine games, brought them within six and one-half games of the Giants. On August 10 Boston passed Chicago and St. Louis to capture second place. A sweep of the Giants, climaxed by an extra-inning 1-0 defeat of Christy Mathewson, lopped another three games off the Braves' deficit. A contemporary Boston writer explained how the seemingly powerless Braves continued to win by saying that they had "not been hitting like a flock of Ty Cobbs, but the boys seem to have the punch in the close games." Finally, Boston moved past New York into first place for good on September 8. Stallings drove his team to 94 wins and a 10½ game lead over the Giants.

The 1914 Braves had one more dramatic upset in them. Behind the pitching of James, Rudolph, and Lefty Tyler (who combined for a 1.15 ERA) and the hitting of Evers, Maranville, and catcher Hank Gowdy, Boston demolished the mighty Philadelphia Athletics dynasty in four games. A's owner Connie Mack was infuriated and reacted by selling off most of his stars and condemning his team to seven straight last-place finishes.

Johnny Evers (top), the NL MVP in 1914, hit just .276 but led all league second basemen in fielding. Although he was only age 31, it was his last full season. The 1914 Boston Braves (bottom) and their manager, George Stallings, were the first team to make extensive use of platooning.

Connie Mack breaks up the A's

Between 1910 and 1914, Philadelphia Athletics' manager/part-owner Connie Mack had built a dynasty that won four AL pennants in five seasons around second baseman Eddie Collins, third baseman Home Run Baker, and pitchers Eddie Plank and Chief Bender. When the 1914 Miracle Braves triumphed in the World Series, however, Mack was so upset that he began dismantling the team piece by piece. He first traded Collins and sold Baker. By the middle of the 1915 season, regulars Eddie Murphy, Jack Barry, and Bob Shawkey were traded or sold. Plank and Bender defected to the new Federal League.

Mack was reputed to be a great teacher, and he might have believed that he could make any young fellow a professional baseball player. At any rate, his impulsive player decisions fated the A's to last-place finishes for the next seven years.

EDDIE COLLINS'S
DASH HOME WINS SERIES

Eddie Collins

John McGraw's 1917 Giants continued two great New York traditions: losing the World Series to the American League and producing a celebrated goat.

This time, at least, the Giants did not come into the Series as the favorite. Without big-name starters and with a makeshift offense incorporating Heinie Zimmerman, Benny Kauff, and George Burns, the 1917 pennant-winner was perhaps McGraw's finest managerial hour. His postseason opponent was a budding Chicago dynasty that, after two years as runner-up to Boston, had put together an offensive and defensive powerhouse. Led by outfielder Shoeless Joe Jackson, second baseman Eddie Collins, catcher Ray Schalk, third baseman Buck Weaver, and first baseman Chick Gandil—and on the pitching side, the 28-12 Eddie Cicotte, Lefty Williams, and spitballer Red Faber—the White Sox led the AL in runs scored and ERA, finishing 100-54 to beat Boston by nine games.

In the World Series, Cicotte won game one in Chicago 2-1 on Happy Felsch's fourth-inning home run. Each home team continued to win through game five, with the Sox leading 3-2. The Series moved to New York for game six. Faber and New York's Rube Benton matched scoreless innings until the fourth inning, when the ghosts of Fred Merkle and Fred Snodgrass again seemed to haunt the Giants. Leadoff batter Collins sent an ordinary grounder to third baseman Zimmerman, who wildly overthrew first and put Collins on second base. Next, Dave Robertson muffed Jackson's easy fly to right, putting White Sox on first and third. Felsch was the third Chicago batter to attempt to make an out, this time by a dribbler back to the pitcher, but to no avail. Benton saw Collins break for home, started a rundown, and threw the ball to Zimmerman, who turned to fire the ball to—nobody. Catcher Bill Rariden was backing up third and neither Benton nor first baseman Walter Holke was covering the plate. Zimmerman had no choice but to run after the speedy Collins, who scored easily. Chicago went on to win the game and the Series, 4-2. Zimmerman could hardly be blamed for not being able to cover two bases at once, but as author of the error that had put the go-ahead run on base, he was the easy selection as Series goat. Undoubtedly, the ridiculous sight of his futile chase after Collins also contributed.

The 1917 Series and the Giants' climactic sixth-game collapse brought together a number of key figures in the eruption of gambling scandals that changed baseball forever in 1919. The 1917 White Sox were virtually identical to the infamous 1919 Black Sox and were already divided into the factions—one led by the college-educated Collins and the other by the corrupt Gandil. Giants third baseman Heinie Zimmerman was also banned for life for throwing games.

Heinie Zimmerman, shown here at the plate, was characterized as the fall guy after he lost the foot race with Eddie Collins as Collins was able to score easily in the 1917 fall classic. Although Zimmerman was the lone third baseman to win a major league batting crown prior to 1949, Giant manager John McGraw jettisoned him after the 1919 season.

TWO HURLERS VIE IN 26-INNING TIE

Joe Oeschger (top),
Leon Cadore

According to most baseball historians, by 1920 the pitching-dominated dead-ball days were over. If that is so, then someone must have forgotten to tell the Boston Braves or the Brooklyn Robins. On May 1 of that year, Boston and Brooklyn played the deadest game in dead-ball history, a 26-inning 1-1 tie.

"From 3 o'clock until near 7 in the evening" led the *Boston Post* the next day, and proceeded to give its readers the shocking news that the game had taken three hours and 50 minutes to play 26 innings. Today, nine innings can take that long. The game's low walk and strikeout totals (nine and 14, respectively) show that the pitchers, in true dead-ball fashion, were throwing strikes. That only two runs were scored on 25 hits shows why; with an extremely high proportion of all hits being singles, dead-ball era pitchers were free to put the ball in play without risking a game-breaking home run. This obviously speeds up play, allowing an average of less than nine minutes per inning.

Most amazing, though, is the fact that both teams' starting pitchers, Leon Cadore for the Robins and Joe Oeschger for the Braves, pitched all 26 innings. This was unusual even for those days of iron-man heroics; neither starting catcher went the distance. Strangely enough, Oeschger had survived a 20-inning game the year before and perhaps the experience helped; the veteran righthander allowed a mere nine hits and in only one inning, the 17th, did Brooklyn put two hits together in an inning. Cadore lived a little more dangerously, allowing 15 hits and relying on his superb defense to bail him out of trouble. With one out in the ninth and the bases loaded, second baseman Ivy Olson killed a Boston rally by fielding a grounder, tagging the runner going by, and then getting the force at first. In the sixth, Boston had tied up the score and was threatening to take the lead, but third baseman Tony Boeckel was cut down at the plate by a brilliant relay from the outfield. Boston second baseman Charlie Pick went *0-11*—and two other players took 0-10 line scores.

So it went until umpire William McCormick declared a tie on account of darkness, setting the all-time record for the most innings in a single game. How long could Cadore and Oeschger have gone on? Consider that neither allowed a run over the final 20 innings or even a hit over the final six. Later, Oeschger said that he felt tired after the 18th inning, but his teammates kept telling him "just one more inning, Joe, and we'll get a run." Cadore claimed that his arm could have gone a few more innings, but admitted that by the end he was "growing sleepy."

Joe Oeschger (top),
*who lived to be age 95,
won 20 games the year
following the 26-inning
marathon but declined
precipitously thereafter.
Leon Cadore* (bottom),
*joined the Dodgers late
in 1916 after winning 25
games in the
International League
and collected all of his
68 career wins in
Brooklyn garb.*

WAMBSGANSS GETS TRIPLE PLAY IN WORLD SERIES

Bill Wambsganss

Cleveland won its first pennant in 1920. Led by outfielder/manager Tris Speaker (who hit .388 with 50 doubles), Elmer Smith, and Larry Gardner, the Indians had the AL's top offense with 857 runs. Their pitching staff featured the 31-game winner Jim Bagby and Stan Coveleski, as well as the formidable duo of Ray Caldwell (20-10) and "Duster" Mails, who had a 7-0 record with a 1.85 ERA.

But the Indians' success was overshadowed by a pair of other historic occurrences: the Black Sox scandal and the death of Cleveland shortstop Ray Chapman, killed by a pitch from Yankee Carl Mays. Both tragedies affected the outcome of the pennant race, as Joe Sewell brilliantly replaced Chapman at short while Chicago and New York faded to finish two and three games respectively behind the Indians.

Wilbert Robinson's Brooklyn Robins won the National pennant behind spitballer Burleigh Grimes and hosted Cleveland in game one of the best five-of-nine series on October 5. Coveleski defeated former Giant ace Rube Marquard 3-1. After Grimes and Sherry Smith beat Bagby and Caldwell in games two and three, Coveleski won his second of three victories to even things at two-all.

The Indians extended their theme of famous firsts in game five, the turning point of the Series. Elmer Smith took Grimes deep with the bases loaded in the opening inning for the first grand slam in World Series history. The score remained 4-0 until Indians starter Bagby added a three-run shot in the fourth, the first World Series home run by a pitcher. Brooklyn rallied in the fifth after lead-off hitter Pete Kilduff reached on a hit and catcher Otto Miller singled him to second with none out. The stage was now set for Cleveland's greatest first of all.

With lefthanded relief pitcher Clarence Mitchell up next, Robinson decided against a pinch hitter; Mitchell could hit, going six for 18 that season as a pinch hitter himself. Expecting him to pull the righty Bagby, second baseman Bill Wambsganss moved back onto the outfield grass and toward first. Mitchell, however, lined a shot up the middle to his backhand side and both runners took off. Wambsganss lunged, made the catch, and let his momentum carry him to second base for the easy second out. Then he turned, saw a stunned Miller standing a few feet away, and applied the tag for the third out. It took the Cleveland crowd a few seconds to grasp that they had just seen the first World Series triple play.

Brooklyn's luck didn't change in the rest of the Series—they were shut out in games six and seven—and neither did Mitchell's. His next time up, he grounded into a double play, to account for 19 percent of his team's outs in only two at-bats.

Jim Bagby (top) *was the only 30-game winner who never won 20 before his big season or after it.* Bottom: *Bill Wambsganss tagging out a dumbstruck Otto Miller to complete his triple play. Ironically, Wambsganss (his name was shortened to Wamby in box scores) led all American League second basemen in errors in 1920.*

Ray Chapman

Carl Mays's pitch kills Ray Chapman

Despite more than a century of brushbacks, beanballs, bruises, and concussions, only one man has ever been killed by a major league pitch.

The death of Ray Chapman in 1920 was a terrible accident—he seemed to have lost sight of the worn, discolored baseball as it sped toward his skull—but it was not entirely bad luck. Chapman used to crowd the plate as a tactic, and Carl Mays threw a lot of knock-down pitches. This incident left a lasting impact on the game in that it was used as an excuse by the leagues to order umpires to keep new, white baseballs in play and to prohibit white-shirted fans from sitting in center field. These changes are underrated factors in the home run explosion of the 1920s.

Bagby
P. Cleveland Amer.

SENATORS TAKE SERIES ON BAD HOP

The 1924 World Series entailed the novelty of the perennially weak Washington Senators making it to their first World Series. There was also the more familiar penchant of the New York Giants for the well-timed calamity.

The Senators had the great Walter Johnson—now 36 years old and still leading the AL in strikeouts, wins, shutouts, and ERA. In game one, Art Nehf faced Johnson and led 2-1 after eight and one-half innings, but shortstop Roger Peckinpaugh doubled in a run in the bottom of the ninth. Both pitchers battled until the 12th, when the Giants scored twice and barely held on in the bottom of the inning to win 4-3. The two teams traded victories through game five, when Johnson's poor 13-hit, three-strikeout performance made him 0-2 and put his team down in the Series 3-2. But Tom Zachary defeated Nehf 2-1 in game six to set up a seventh-game matchup between New York's number-three starter Virgil Barnes and righty spot-starter Curly Ogden.

Starting the unsung Ogden turned out to be a trick by Washington manager Bucky Harris to get the platooned lefty Bill Terry into the starting lineup. Short on lefthanded pitching, Harris knew he would have to go to his righthanders in the late innings and didn't want the dangerous Terry in John McGraw's arsenal of pinch hitters. After two batters, Harris removed Ogden for lefty George Mogridge, who pitched effectively through the sixth, when the Giants rallied and McGraw pinch-hit for Terry with Irish Meusel. Harris's ploy had worked, but Meusel drove in a run and the Giants scored two more to take a 3-1 lead. Barnes coasted into the eighth, when he walked the bases loaded with two out for Bucky Harris. Harris bounced to third, but the ball hopped crazily up over Lindstrom's head to score the tying runs.

Harris brought in Johnson in the ninth. With one last chance at a World Series win, the "Big Train" came through, striking out five and scattering three hits over four innings. In the bottom of the 12th with one out, the Senators threatened. Muddy Ruel popped up but catcher Hank Gowdy tossed away his face mask, then, comically, caught his spikes in it—twice—and let the ball drop. Ruel doubled. Johnson then reached base on a Travis Jackson error. Still, Fate was not done with the Giants. Earl McNeely followed with a double-play ball right at Lindstrom but, incredibly, the ball took another crazy hop, landing in left field as Ruel crossed the plate with the winning run.

Four of the seven games in the 1924 Series were decided by one run and two lasted 12 innings. New York scored 27 runs on 66 hits; Washington scored 26 runs on 61 hits. Giants pitchers walked 29 and struck out 34, while Washington walked 25 and struck out 40.

Earl McNeely slides safely into third during the fourth game of the 1924 World Series (top). McNeely was a rookie in 1924. Fred Lindstrom (bottom) was the youngest man to participate in a World Series as a regular player. He was only age 18 when a pebble victimized him and made McNeely a hero.

PIRATES COME BACK FROM THREE-GAME SERIES DEFICIT

Roger Peckinpaugh

The 1925 World Series was a mirror image of the 1924 Series. Like the previous year's edition, this Series went seven tense games. It was punctuated by great plays—such as Sam Rice's catch—and great lapses, such as 1925 AL MVP Roger Peckinpaugh's eight errors. Washington's luck completely reversed; in 1925, it was the Senators, rather than their opponents, who were undone by clutch misplays and poor field conditions. After a season in which he had gone 20-7 with a 3.07 ERA in a tremendous hitters' year, the ageless Walter Johnson won his first two Series starts over the Pittsburgh Pirates by a combined score of 8-1 before losing the seventh and deciding game.

The Series began well enough for Washington, whose only loss through game four came on an unearned run when Peckinpaugh booted an easy grounder. Besides Johnson, the hero of the Series to that point was Washington outfielder Sam Rice. In the eighth inning of game three with a 4-3 lead, manager Bucky Harris moved Rice into right field as a defensive replacement for Joe Harris, who had driven in the lead run in the seventh. With two outs, lefthand-hitting Pirate catcher Earl Smith whacked a drive toward the temporary bleachers in right that looked sure to tie the game. But Rice sped to the three-foot wall, leaped, crashed, and fell into the first row of seats. Umpire Cy Rigler ran to the outfield and waited a full 10 seconds—as Rice untangled himself from the crowd to finally emerge with the baseball in his glove—before calling Smith out. Pittsburgh manager Bill McKechnie went crazy, but the call stood. Thereafter, whenever Rice was asked whether he had really made the catch, he would smile and say only "the umpire said I did." Rice's reticence continued until after his death until 1974, when a sealed letter was discovered in which he finally revealed what had happened: Although he was momentarily dazed after banging his throat on a seat, he had made a clean catch and kept "a death grip" on the ball.

Down 3-1, the Pirates came back on Aldridge's 6-3 win in game five. Peckinpaugh made a critical error in game six that led to Washington's 3-2 loss. One unkind writer suggested that Peckinpaugh was campaigning for NL MVP as well.

Game seven was played in an increasingly heavy rain and on a field that by game's end was completely covered with mud. Only the Senators seemed to be affected. Johnson pitched slowly, as though he couldn't find his footing on the mound, and squandered leads of 4-0, 6-3, and 7-6 on the way to giving up 15 hits. Peckinpaugh outdid himself, committing two more errors as Pittsburgh rallied for five runs in the last two innings to win 9-7. Only five of the runs were earned.

Sam Rice warming up while Roger Peckinpaugh looks on. Rice led the Senators to the fall classic with a .350 average and 227 base hits. He set a record with 12 base hits in the '25 Series. Rice hit .349 with 207 hits at age 40 in 1930, five years after he made his fabled catch.

Pie Traynor

One of the stars of the 1925 Pirates was Pie Traynor, who batted .320 during the season and .346 in the Series with two triples.

Usually batting fifth in the Pirates order, Traynor batted .320 lifetime with seven 100-RBI seasons and led NL third basemen in putouts seven times, stats which prompted later generations to consider him the greatest third baseman between the World Wars. *The Sporting News* put him on their All-Star team six times from 1925 to 1933. Although Traynor's numbers are no better than above-average for hitters of his time, they were tops among third basemen of his time. He was never a threat to lead the NL in hitting, or anything else besides triples, and he lacked both extraordinary power and towering on-base averages.

PETE ALEXANDER STRIKES OUT TONY LAZZERI TO SECURE SERIES

Grover Cleveland "Pete" Alexander

Over his 20-year career, Grover Cleveland "Pete" Alexander won 373 games, including eight 20-win seasons and three 30-victory campaigns. But despite all those wins, the greatest moment of his Hall of Fame career came when he saved a game as a relief pitcher during the 1926 World Series between the St. Louis Cardinals and the New York Yankees.

At the beginning of the '26 season, the man who in his prime had been called "Alex the Great" was considered "'Old Pete' the has-been." He had spent time that winter in a sanatorium due to epilepsy and alcohol abuse. He was age 39 when he reported to spring training with the Cubs. But Alexander broke his ankle during camp, argued with manager Joe McCarthy once the season started, and was released by June.

When it appeared his career was over, Cardinals player/manager Rogers Hornsby plucked Alexander from the scrap heap and put him into the Cards' rotation. Alexander gave to "The Rajah" everything that he had left in his aging right arm, producing nine victories and helping the Redbirds to their first pennant and a World Series meeting with the Yankees.

After the Cardinals lost game one of the Series, Alexander brought his team back with a 6-2 win, retiring the last 21 Yankees in order. When the Bronx Bombers won two of the next three games, it was up to Alexander to keep his team in the Series. He came through with a 10-2 victory and, legend has it, did a hefty amount of drinking that night, confident his work for the Series was over.

In the deciding seventh game, Jesse Haines pitched the Cardinals to a 3-2 lead after six innings. But with two out in the seventh frame, Haines suddenly walked the bases loaded. Up next for the Yanks was the year's outstanding rookie Tony Lazzeri, who during the regular season was second on the team to Babe Ruth in RBI with 114.

Hornsby remembered that Alexander had struck out Lazzeri four times the day before and, to the amazement of 38,093 fans in Yankee Stadium, called Alex in from the bullpen to stop the Yankee threat. After one ball, Lazzeri missed at a curve. The next pitch was a fastball and Lazzeri hit a line drive that was almost a homer but veered just a few feet foul. On the next delivery, Alex went back to his curve ball and Lazzeri went down on strikes—again.

The Yankees would not threaten to score again. Alexander kept the Yankees off of the bases until two out in the ninth, when he walked Babe Ruth. Ruth uncharacteristically tried to steal second and was thrown out. Alexander saved the game and the Cardinals won the Series.

Old Pete Alexander, picked up in 1926 to pitch as a Cardinal, struck out Tony Lazzeri with bases loaded and two out in inning eight of game seven of the Series, one of the most famous at-bats in Series history. Alexander won 21 for the Birds in 1927 when he was age 40, relying on memory and cunning—he fanned just 48 hitters in 268 innings.

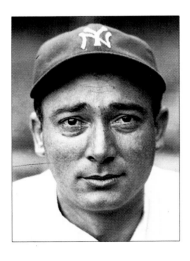

Tony Lazzeri

Tony Lazzeri may be remembered most for being Pete Alexander's key strikeout victim in the last game of the 1926 World Series, but Yankee fans remember him for being the greatest second baseman in the team's history. In his 1926 rookie season, Lazzeri batted .275 with 18 homers and 114 RBI, and a year later was part of the famed Murderer's Row. Though Babe Ruth and Lou Gehrig received all the acclaim on that club, Lazzeri contributed a .309 average, 18 homers, and 102 RBI. He remained the club's second baseman for the next 10 seasons and was voted the best at his position in 1932. Lazzeri was also one of New York's most popular players. When he batted at Yankee Stadium, the fans would yell his nickname, "Poosh 'Em Up," urging their hero to hit them a ball in the stands. Lazzeri regularly did.

BABE RUTH'S
60 HOME RUNS

Not counting his short but impressive early stint as a pitcher with the Boston Red Sox, Babe Ruth's career reached not one, but two peaks. After setting new home run records with 11 in 1918, 29 in 1919, 54 as a Yankee in 1920, and, finally, 59 in 1921, Ruth had revolutionized baseball and set a standard no succeeding slugger has been able to match. The legendary "Bambino" made home run-hitting one of those rare arts—like epic poetry and tragedy—whose earliest practitioners are ranked by posterity as the greatest.

Ruth faded a bit in his late 20s, perhaps worn down by drinking, partying, and general excess as well as his frequent squabbles with Yankee management and the Commissioner. His home run totals dropped into the 40s in 1923, '24, and '26 and below in 1922 when he was suspended for illegal barnstorming, and in 1925, when stomach surgery and another suspension limited him to 98 games.

However, those who thought that he might be through were mistaken. In 1927, at the age of 32, Ruth hit his 60th home run of the season off pitcher Tom Zachary (who had also given up numbers 22 and 36) to reach his greatest home run total ever. His major league record stood for 32 years, until Roger Maris hit 61 homers in 1961. Ruth also batted .356 with 138 walks, 158 runs scored, and 164 RBI.

Ruth may well have been spurred on by the competition of budding Yankee power-hitter Lou Gehrig, then in his third full season and batting behind Ruth in the clean-up slot. In 1927, the 24-year-old first baseman who had never hit more than 20 home runs or batted over .313 hit .373, drove in a league-high 175 runs, and nearly kept pace with Ruth in home runs until September, when Ruth put on a unique long-ball stretch drive by swatting 17 (including three on September 6 and two each on the September 7, 13, and 29). In an historical sense, however, Ruth's competition was never with anyone but himself. And if even he could not duplicate his amazing 1920 and 1921 seasons—the only years in baseball history in which he or anyone else has slugged over .800—the resurgent Babe of 1927 came close, with a .772 mark. In 1961, Roger Maris, by comparison, slugged only .620. Ruth's 60 homers in 1927 represented 38 percent of the Yankees' AL-leading total and 14 percent of the entire league's total—*more than any other single team.* After Gehrig's 47 home runs, third place went to Tony Lazzeri, who hit 18. These awesome numbers are surpassed only by the Ruth of 1920, who hit 47 percent of his team's homers and 15 percent of the league's. Second to his 54 home runs was George Sisler with a mere 19.

Babe Ruth at the finish of one of his mighty swings, watching one of his 60 homers go out. Ruth all by himself out-homered every other American League team in 1927. His .487 on-base percentage that year is number 33 on the all-time list, and it was only his eighth best. His .772 slugging average is number three on the all-time list and was his third best.

Lou Gehrig

Murderer's Row

It's hard to say which was worse news for Yankee opponents in 1927: The New Yorkers' frightening offense, nicknamed "Five O'Clock Lightning" or "Murderer's Row"—which scored 975 runs, batted .307, and led the AL in hits, triples, homers, and walks—or their overlooked but awesome pitching staff. Waite Hoyt, Wilcy Moore, Herb Pennock, & Co. matched Ruth and Gehrig in their own department, leading the league in fewest runs, hits, and walks and in ERA at 3.20.

Yankee foes had another problem. The Yankees sought to avenge their loss in the 1926 World Series. They first whipped the American League by winning 110 games and finishing 19 games ahead of a good Philadelphia club, then humiliated the poor Pirates in the Series in a four-game sweep.

A's 10-RUN INNING IN WORLD SERIES

Jimmie Foxx

Fifteen years after the disastrous sweep by the "Miracle Braves" of 1914, Connie Mack returned to the postseason stage with a power-packed team including such hitters as Jimmie Foxx, Mule Haas, Al Simmons, and Mickey Cochrane. Led by George Earnshaw at 24-8, 18-game winner Rube Walberg, and ERA-leader Lefty Grove at 20-6, the deep Athletics staff also compiled the league's best ERA (3.44).

Going into the World Series against Chicago, however, Mack was worried about the Cubs' fearsome righthand-hitting attack. The 1929 Cubs destroyed lefthanded fastball pitchers, and Grove and Walberg were just that. During the season, second baseman Rogers Hornsby batted .380 with 39 homers and 156 runs scored; the Chicago outfield of Kiki Cuyler, Hack Wilson, and Riggs Stephenson hit .362 collectively with 337 runs and 271 RBI. They were all righthanders.

Mack, a veteran of 44 seasons, made one of the most daring strategic moves in Series history: He put Grove and Walberg in the bullpen and in game one started 35-year-old righty Howard Ehmke, who had made only 11 appearances on the season. Ehmke struck out a Series-record 13, and scattered eight hits and a walk to win 3-1. Another veteran righty, George Earnshaw, started the next two games, winning game two 9-3 and losing game three 3-1.

Mack started ancient spitballer Jack Quinn in game four. Quinn may have been righthanded—and he quite literally threw junk—but he failed to match Ehmke's success, allowing six runs before being lifted in the sixth.

The 29,921 fans were filing out of the original Shibe Park as Cubs starter Charlie Root brought an 8-0 lead to the bottom of the seventh. He lost the shutout in the instant it took one of his high fastballs to rocket off the bat of leadoff hitter Al Simmons onto the left field roof. Jimmie Foxx then singled. The next batter, Bing Miller, flied to Hack Wilson in center, but Wilson lost the ball in the sun and let it drop. Suddenly, the roof caved in on the Chicago pitching staff; Nehf entered the game with the score 8-4, two men on, and Mule Haas at the plate. Haas smacked the first pitch on a line toward Wilson, who looked up and saw nothing. By the time the ball could be retrieved from deep center field, all three men had scored to make it 8-7. A base on balls later, Sheriff Blake came in for Nehf, but was tagged for two hits and a run. Pat Malone finally ended the inning, but not before allowing runs number nine and 10 on Jimmy Dykes's bases-loaded double to complete the greatest single-game comeback in World Series history. The A's won the game 10-8 and, behind Ehmke and Walberg in game five, defeated the shell-shocked Cubs 3-2 on three runs in the ninth inning.

Al Simmons beats out an infield hit. The AL RBI leader in 1929, he also enjoyed the first of five consecutive campaigns in which he collected 200 or more hits. Dissimilarly, Mule Haas hit two home runs to shatter the Cubs' hopes of pulling out the 1929 Series; the following year Haas hit just two homers all season.

Howard Ehmke

Ehmke's surprise start

Even though Howard Ehmke is "Howard Who?" in the anecdotal history of the 1929 World Series, he was not a nobody in his day. A 116-116 pitcher over 15 seasons, Ehmke pitched a no-hitter in 1923 and in his next start came within one controversial infield hit of gaining the first back-to-back no-hitters.

Connie Mack is said to have been intrigued by the success that Rube Ehrhardt, a Cincinnati pitcher with a style similar to control artist Ehmke's, had had against the Cubs. So Mack, secretly planning on starting Ehmke in game one, dropped him out of the rotation in the final weeks of the season and sent him to study the Chicago hitters.

HACK WILSON'S EPIC SEASON

Although the home run era may have begun in 1920, its effects continued throughout the Roaring Twenties, as the number of runs scored shot up year after year until 1930. The baseball was deadened the next season, ensuring that 1930 would go down in history—20th-century history, at least—as the absolute peak of the batting outburst.

It was fun while it lasted. The American League batted .288; the National, .303; AL pitchers compiled an ERA of 4.65; NL hurlers, an ugly 4.97. The St. Louis Cardinals finished first with an ERA of 4.40 and 1,004 runs scored. Incredibly, last-place Philadelphia outhit them .315 to .314. The lopsided Phillies had two .380 hitters in their lineup (Chuck Klein and Lefty O'Doul), but their pitchers allowed 1,199 runs and had an ERA of 6.71. A short list of individual single-season hitting records set in 1930 would comprise five of the all-time top 50 seasons in batting average, five of the top 25 in RBI, five of the top 25 in total bases, four of the top 20 in slugging average, and two of the top 10 in home runs.

If Ty Cobb was the symbol of the dead-ball era and Babe Ruth the hero of 1920, the personification of 1930 was the wild Lewis "Hack" Wilson. The free-swinging, home run bashing, and utterly eccentric Chicago Cubs center fielder put together one of the few National League seasons that can be compared with the best of Ruth and Lou Gehrig. A legendary drinker and carouser who was once reprimanded by Commissioner Kenesaw Mountain Landis reputedly for socializing with Al Capone, the 5'6", 220-pound barrel-chested and spindly-legged slugger, after failing to impress the New York Giants, came to Chicago in 1926. There he blossomed, batting over .300 and upping his home run totals each year until 1930.

Wilson had an overwhelming year in 1930. He drove in a major league-record *190* RBI, clobbered a National League-record 56 home runs, drew 105 walks, and scored 146 runs. He batted .356 and slugged .723. If not the National League's best hitter that year—an argument could be made for Chuck Klein—he was the most flamboyant. Chicago fans reveled in the sight of the comically stubby Wilson wildly flailing at the ball with his favored 40-ounce tree trunk of a bat. In the spirit of the times in which he lived, Hack swung away with abandon.

Only a year later, Wilson's day was over. His hitting fell off even more drastically than the rest of the league's, to only 13 home runs and a .261 batting average. By 1934, he was out of baseball at age 34; 14 years later, he was dead.

Hack Wilson takes a cut (top). Batting ahead of Wilson in the Cubs' order, Kiki Cuyler and Woody English scored 307 runs between them in 1930. Wilson and Cuyler combined to knock in 324 runs, breaking an NL record that Wilson and Rogers Hornsby set in 1929. Wilson was capable in center field (bottom), though he led NL outfielders in errors in 1930.

PEPPER MARTIN SECURES WORLD SERIES

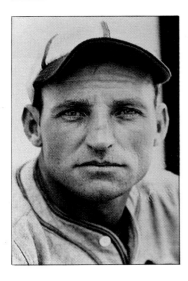

The 1931 World Series pitting the St. Louis Cardinals against the Philadelphia Athletics powerhouse—Al Simmons, Jimmie Foxx, Mickey Cochrane, and pitcher Lefty Grove—was supposed to crown the Athletics as champions for the third successive year. It, instead, became a showcase for the 27-year-old Cardinals center fielder, Pepper Martin.

John Leonard Roosevelt Martin starred in the minor leagues for seven seasons before cracking the Cardinals' starting lineup in '31. A writer once described him as "a chunky, unshaven hobo who ran the bases like a berserk locomotive, slept in the raw, and swore at pitchers in his sleep." Making up in effort what he lacked in ability, Martin batted .300 his first season, becoming an inspiration to Depression-era fans with his fearless outfield play and headfirst slides.

Pepper also fired up the underdog Cardinals in the Series. The Athletics won the first game 6-2 behind Grove, but Martin went 3-for-4 and stole a base. Pepper almost single-handedly won game two, creating both runs in the 2-0 victory with daring baserunning. In the second inning, he stretched a single into a double, stole third, and scored on a sacrifice fly. In the seventh, he singled, stole second, went to third on a ground out, and scored on a squeeze bunt. In game three, Martin led the Cardinals to a 5-2 win, going 2-for-4 and scoring two runs against Grove. Although the Athletics tied the Series in game four behind George Earnshaw's two-hit shutout, Pepper remained hot, knocking both Cardinal hits.

Martin really put on a show in the fifth game. He drove in a run with a sacrifice fly in the first inning, beat out a bunt in the fourth, knocked a two-run homer in the sixth, and delivered an RBI single in the eighth. Martin's four RBI led the Cardinals to a 5-1 victory and a 3-2 lead in the Series. After five games, Pepper had a .667 batting average (12-for-18), five runs scored, four doubles, one homer, five RBI, and four stolen bases.

Philadelphia tied the Series, winning game six 8-1, but that couldn't sap the momentum that Martin gave the Cardinals. St. Louis won game seven at home, 4-2. Though Pepper went hitless in the last two games, he halted a ninth-inning Athletics rally in the final game with a sprinting shoestring catch of a line drive.

Called "The Wild Horse of the Osage," Martin became a World Series hero again in 1934. With 11 hits in that seven-game Series victory over the Detroit Tigers, Martin ended his career with a record .418 World Series batting average. He will, however, be remembered for the '31 Series—what the legendary baseball writer Red Smith called "the greatest one-man show the baseball world has ever known."

Pepper Martin at bat in the 1931 World Series (top); the A's catcher is Mickey Cochrane. Martin's emergence in 1931 made crack center fielder Taylor Douthit expendable—he was traded to Cincinnati. Bottom: Al Simmons being congratulated at home plate by Jimmie Foxx after hitting a two-run homer to spoil Burleigh Grimes's shutout in game three.

RUTH'S CALLED SHOT

The 1932 World Series seized a place in baseball history for a single incident: Babe Ruth's supposed "called shot" home run off Cubs pitcher Charlie Root. Like so many other Ruth anecdotes, this one grows blurrier upon closer inspection. Regardless of its veracity, the story does reflect a broader truth—that the myth of the mighty Babe transcended baseball.

Ruth had a good year in 1932, hitting .341 with 41 home runs. However, Philadelphia's Jimmie Foxx led the American League in homers, the first time that someone other than the Babe had won the homer crown since he had stomach problems in 1925. The Bronx Bombers still had the most powerful offense in baseball, however. They scored 1,002 runs, won 107 games, and left Foxx and the A's 13 games in the dust. In the Series, the Yankees steamed over the Chicago Cubs in four straight, outscoring them 37-19; none of the games was closer than two runs.

Ruth's disputed feat came at one of the few close moments in the World Series—with the score tied 4-4 in the fifth inning of game three. This was the first game in Chicago, and the fans, smelling disaster, were in an ugly mood. So were the players, although for different reasons. The Yankees felt that their skipper, Joe McCarthy, had been badly treated when he was fired by Chicago two years before, and they said so publicly. They also resented the Cubs for voting only a half-share in the Series money to former Yankee shortstop Mark Koenig, who had been traded to Chicago for the stretch drive and hit .353.

When Ruth came to bat, then, all kinds of abuse rained down on him from the stands. The Cubs bench jockeys hurled insults and Ruth answered back as he stepped in and took Root's first pitch for a strike; some said they then saw him hold up one finger. Two balls later, he looked at strike two and again appeared to make some kind of gesture. Finally, Ruth swung and knocked a loud two-run homer into the center field bleachers.

These are more or less the facts. There are, however, as many different accounts as witnesses. Root always fiercely denied that any "call" had taken place. If it had, he insisted, Ruth would have been digging ball three out of his ear. Ruth himself was just as adamant in refusing to confirm or deny a thing. On-deck hitter Lou Gehrig and at least one sportswriter, however, said that they were sure they saw Babe point out where and when he was going to hit a home run and then proceed to deliver. Fact or fabrication, the myth lives on.

Robert Thom's painting of Babe Ruth's famed "Called Shot." The piece hangs in the Hall of Fame. No photograph of the moment exists— perhaps because it never occurred. Ruth did hit the home run off of Charlie Root in the fifth inning, his second of game three. Lou Gehrig followed with a shot of his own, his second smash of the game.

CARL HUBBELL FANS FIVE STRAIGHT HALL OF FAMERS

The midsummer classic between the AL and NL in 1934 was titled "The Game of the Century." It had been inaugurated the year before as a gimmick to hype Chicago's World's Fair and to build circulation for the *Chicago Tribune,* whose sports editor, Arch Ward, conceived the idea. Babe Ruth's two-run homer had won the first "exhibition" for the American League, 4-2, and the National League sought to avenge the loss in the second game held at New York's Polo Grounds.

New York Giants manager Bill Terry selected his ace pitcher, "King Carl" Hubbell, as the NL's starter in front of his home fans. The lefthanded Hubbell had won the Most Valuable Player Award in 1933, leading the league in wins, ERA, and shutouts. Hubbell's "out" pitch was the baffling screwball, which broke away from righthanded hitters and in on lefties.

"The Meal Ticket," as Hubbell was also called, would need all his pitches working splendidly when facing the AL's power-laden lineup, which looked more like a future Hall of Fame honor roll—Charlie Gehringer, Heinie Manush, Babe Ruth, Lou Gehrig, Jimmie Foxx, Al Simmons, Joe Cronin, and Bill Dickey.

Before the game, Hubbell huddled with his catcher, Gabby Hartnett of the Chicago Cubs. "They've never seen a screwball like you have before," Hartnett told Hubbell. "We'll waste everything except the screwball."

It initially appeared as if the strategy would backfire, as Hubbell got into trouble before many of the 48,363 fans could get comfortable. Gehringer lined the first pitch into center for a single, and after Hubbell got ahead of Manush 0-2, he walked him on the next four pitches—not what a pitcher wants to do with Ruth, Gehrig, and Foxx next in line.

Hubbell fell behind Ruth, 1-0, then broke three straight screwballs over the heart of the plate. Next up was Gehrig, the most feared RBI man in the game. On one and two, the "Iron Horse" swung so hard missing a screwball that he almost screwed himself into the ground. The powerful righthanded-hitting Foxx didn't fare any better. After two frustrating screwballs at the knees, his immense swing at the third almost caused him to fall down.

In the second inning, with his team up 1-0, Hubbell faced Simmons, who was known to talk himself into a hitting frenzy. A few Hubbell scroogies later, Simmons was talking to himself as he walked to the bench. When the Washington Senator player/manager Joe Cronin also went down on strikes, Hubbell had whiffed five of the game's greatest hitters in succession. Dickey ended the streak with a single.

The AL eventually won the contest, 9-7, scoring all their runs in the three innings after Hubbell departed. The outcome mattered little, however; this game belonged to Hubbell.

Carl Hubbell uncorks a screwball in the 1936 World Series. The screwball is one of the most difficult pitches to hit because it acts like a reverse curveball. Rather than moving towards a righthanded batter as a lefty's curve does, the "scroogie" moves away from a righty batter.

DIZZY DEAN'S
30-WIN SEASON

In his first two seasons pitching for the St. Louis Cardinals, 1931 and 1932, Jay Hannah "Dizzy" Dean won 38 games. With his younger brother Paul (also known as "Daffy") joining the team in 1934, the colorful Dizzy boldly predicted that "Me and Paul will probably win 40 games." As it turned out, Dizzy was a better pitcher than prognosticator. The brother act won almost 50 games. Diz became the premier pitcher in baseball, leading the Cardinals to the National League pennant with 30 victories—no NL pitcher since has won that many games in a season— and Paul produced 19 wins.

Dean featured an explosive fastball, a tight breaking curve, and excellent command of both pitches. He was as aggressive on the mound as he was fun-loving off it, and he would intimidate hitters by throwing his fastball high and inside. Sometimes he would tell hitters that the heater was coming and still throw it by them.

In '34, Dean's superb pitching kept the Cardinals on the heels of the New York Giants, who led the league for most of the year. Dizzy then sparked a 21-4 September spurt that enabled the Cards to tie the Giants on the 28th. While the Brooklyn Dodgers were beating the Giants, the Cardinals won their last three games—two on shutouts by Dean—to take the pennant. Dizzy was named the Most Valuable Player with his 30 victories (against only seven losses) for an .811 winning percentage. Dizzy also led the league in shutouts (seven) and strikeouts (196). He placed second in ERA (2.65), complete games (24), and games pitched (50). He even kicked in with seven saves out of the bullpen, tying him for second in the NL. Opponents had a .241 batting average and a .286 on-base percentage against Dean, third-best in the league.

Before the World Series against the Detroit Tigers, Dizzy characteristically insisted that "Me 'n' Paul will win two games each." Though Detroit beat Dizzy 3-1 in game five, his victories in games one and seven and Paul's wins in games three and six gave St. Louis its second championship in four years. To those who chided his boastfulness, Dizzy pitched one of his immortal lines: "If you say you're going to do it, and you go out and do it, it ain't bragging."

Dean went out and did it for two more seasons—28 wins in 1935 and 24 in 1936—until a line drive broke his toe in the 1937 All-Star Game. The foot injury forced him to alter his pitching delivery, which subsequently caused a sore arm. Dizzy was never again the same pitcher.

Dizzy Dean would probably be the first to claim that if it hadn't been for a freak injury, he would have compiled the best statistics of any pitcher in baseball history. And he might have been right. A man with boundless self-confidence, Dean was baseball's most colorful player. In 1934, he became the NL's first 30-game winner in 17 years.

Joe "Ducky" Medwick

Gas House Gang

Manager Frank Frisch piloted an irascible, gritty, aggressive group of St. Louis Cardinals known as the "Gas House Gang."

The rest of the colorful cast of characters on those Redbird teams included the boastful pitcher Dizzy Dean, the hustling outfielder Joe "Ducky" Medwick, fiery outfielder Pepper Martin, and the hard-nosed shortstop Leo "The Lip" Durocher.

The Gas House Gang won a memorable seven-game World

Series in 1934 against Detroit. In game seven, Medwick aroused the Tiger fans' wrath by sliding hard into Detroit third baseman Marv Owen during a 9-0 Cards win. When he returned to the outfield in the sixth inning, Detroit fans showered Medwick with fruit, bottles, and other debris. It got so bad, Commissioner Kenesaw Mountain Landis ordered Medwick off the field. By that point, Medwick had already batted .379 and won permanent recognition for the band of feisty players.

JOHNNY VANDER MEER HURLS TWO CONSECUTIVE NO-HITTERS

Perhaps the most unlikely thing about Johnny "Dutch Master" Vander Meer's feat of throwing two successive no-hit games in June of 1938 is that Vander Meer pitched them. First scouted in a New Jersey Sunday School League (where he pitched three consecutive no-hitters), the erratic, fire-balling Vander Meer bounced around the Dodgers' and Braves' minor league systems before landing with the Reds' Durham, North Carolina, farm club. There he struck out 295 in 214 innings. Cincinnati called him up for the 1937 season, putting him under the guidance of manager Bill McKechnie, who worked on developing a more consistent delivery of his impressive fastball. After a 6-10 start in 1938, Vander Meer settled into a winning groove. On June 11, he no-hit the Braves at home, 3-0. He set down the first nine Boston batters in order and then the final 13.

His next start, June 15, 1938, was a sell-out as Brooklyn's Ebbets Field became the second big-league park to host a game of night baseball. How much the brand-new, untested lights contributed to Vander Meer's second no-hitter will never be known. In any case, by the middle innings, the 40,000-strong Brooklyn crowd began to root for Vander Meer, who held the Dodgers to a pair of walks in the seventh inning and breezed along with a 6-0 lead until the ninth. All of a sudden, his wildness returned. He threw three off-target pitches before retiring the leadoff man Buddy Hassett on a dribbler. Eighteen pitches later, Babe Phelps, Cookie Lavagetto, and Dolph Camilli had loaded the bases on free passes and slugging outfielder Ernie Koy was up. But Vander Meer escaped danger as Koy grounded to third baseman Lew Riggs, who threw very carefully to home for the force, and Leo Durocher flied out to short center field.

Even though Vander Meer remained overpowering—he led the NL in strikeouts from 1941 to 1943—he never again pitched as well as he had in the second half of 1938, when he reeled off nine straight wins to finish 15-10 with a 3.12 ERA.

Vander Meer's feat is frequently celebrated as the one major league accomplishment least likely to be outdone. History, however, demonstrates that this just isn't so. Four other pitchers—Allie Reynolds, Virgil Trucks, Jim Maloney, and Nolan Ryan—have thrown two no-hitters in the same season. At least two pitchers have come within one hit of equaling him. In 1923, Howard Ehmke's bid for a second straight no-hitter was ruined by an infield hit that easily could have been ruled an error. Ewell Blackwell came even closer to the record in 1947, giving up a hit in the ninth inning of what would have been his second no-hitter.

Johnny Vander Meer pitches in the first night game in the East (top). He was a hard-throwing but erratic 23-year-old lefthander in only his second major league season with the Reds. Bottom: Vander Meer being escorted off of the field after his second straight no-hitter; he is the player in the middle without the jacket.

Larry MacPhail

Vander Meer's feat boosts night baseball

While night baseball had been technically possible in 1880 (the year two amateur teams played an illuminated game to promote Boston's new electric power company), it took the Depression to convince the tradition-bound major league baseball establishment to try it.

The Reds had drawn only 206,000 fans in all of 1934 when their general manager Larry MacPhail, who had experience with night baseball in the minor leagues, conducted a seven-game experiment under the lights in 1935. The games were a tremendous success. Johnny Vander Meer's second no-hitter came during the first night game played in the East.

Night ball went on even after the Depression. By 1948, every major league park save Wrigley Field had been equipped for night baseball.

GABBY HARTNETT CLOBBERS HOMER IN THE GLOAMIN'

On September 9, 1938, Chicago Cubs catcher Gabby Hartnett found himself living everyone's baseball fantasy: It's the bottom of the ninth in the year's most important game, the score is tied, there are two outs, and it's been announced that the game will be called for darkness after one more batter. Down in the count 0-2, Hartnett swats a curveball deep into the dusk to win the game.

Hartnett's blow was the culmination of a series of improbabilities. He was a veteran catcher near the end of a career that included an MVP Award, a cumulative batting average of .297, and the then records for overall games caught with 1,790 and home runs by a catcher with 236. He was also Cubs owner Philip K. Wrigley's surprise choice to succeed Charlie Grimm as manager in midseason 1938. The move seemed to have no effect on the Cubs, who continued to bring up the rear of a four-team pennant race with the Pirates, Giants, and Reds. The Cubs then began to climb until, after sweeping a Labor Day twin-bill from first-place Pittsburgh, Chicago moved into second place at three and one-half games back. The NL schedule was thrown into chaos by the arrival of a hurricane on the Eastern seaboard. Both teams lost important games to heavy rains, but Pittsburgh was most hurt; the Pirates were washed out of four games against last-place Philadelphia and penultimate Brooklyn. With a week left in the season and its lead down to a game and one-half, Pittsburgh faced Chicago in a decisive three-game showdown. A sore-armed Dizzy Dean somehow lasted into the ninth and won it 2-1.

Game two was a seesaw affair. The Cubs scored one in the first inning, then Pittsburgh's Johnny Rizzo hit a solo homer to tie it in the sixth. In the eighth, the Cubs again fell behind by two runs and again rallied in the bottom of the inning. With the tying runs across and two out, Pirates right fielder Paul Waner cut down the go-ahead run at the plate. The score remained five-all after Charlie Root retired the Pirates in the ninth in increasing darkness. Pittsburgh's Mace Brown got Phil Cavaretta on a fly and Carl Reynolds on a ground out, setting the stage for one of the most storied shots in baseball history. Thanks to some forgotten headline writer's search for another way to say "twilight," the word "gloamin'" has been forever linked to Hartnett.

The Pirates never recovered from Hartnett's homer, losing 10-1 the next day. For the Cubs, the series-sweep capped a 10-game winning streak and a 20-3 pennant stretch drive. In the World Series, however, the Yankees knocked the gloamin' out of Chicago 4-0.

Gabby Hartnett argues with an umpire as Cub manager Charley Grimm runs in to join the fray (top). Hartnett took the managing reins from Grimm in 1938 and guided the Cubs to the pennant. Hartnett crosses the plate following his home run to beat Pittsburgh in the second game of the three-game series sweep (bottom).

LOU GEHRIG'S CONSECUTIVE-GAME STREAK ENDS

Lou Gehrig wore many nicknames during his 15-year career with the New York Yankees between 1925 and 1939, but none fit him better than "The Iron Horse."

From the day he became the Yankees starting first baseman on June 2, 1925 (replacing the injured Wally Pipp), until he removed himself from the lineup on May 2, 1939, Gehrig played in every game, despite illness or injury. He once played the day after being hit so hard on the head with a pitch, it was thought his skull was fractured. On another occasion, when Gehrig felt he couldn't play, manager Joe McCarthy put him first in the line-up as the shortstop, then replaced him in the bottom of the first with Frank Crosetti.

During his 15 years of nonstop playing, Gehrig was a superstar of the era, second only to teammate Babe Ruth. He won the Most Valuable Player Award as a member of the fabled "Murderer's Row" in 1927; won a batting title and Triple Crown in 1934; took the American League home run titles in 1931, '34, and '36; and drove in over 150 runs seven times, still a major league record. He had an AL-record 184 RBI in 1931. Gehrig helped lead the Yankees to six world championships and ranks in the top 10 in 10 World Series hitting departments. Only Ruth had more career home runs than did Gehrig in the late 1930s.

But it was during the 1938 Series, when he batted just .286, that Gehrig's skills showed signs of eroding. In spring training the following year, the 36-year-old Yankee captain's hitting reflexes seemed slow and he didn't move around first base with his usual grace. On May 1, Gehrig was batting under .150 and the day before he had left five men on base. He told McCarthy to scratch him from the lineup for the team's May 2 game in Detroit. When the Yankees were announced without Gehrig's name and Tigers fans were told Lou had voluntarily removed himself from the lineup, Detroit fans gave Gehrig a standing ovation. His amazing, incredible, almost superhuman streak of 2,130 consecutive games played was over.

"Lou just told me he felt it would be best for the club if he took himself out," McCarthy told the press that day.

"It's tough to see your mates on base," Gehrig explained, "have a chance to win a game and not be able to do anything about it."

A few weeks later the world discovered why Gehrig couldn't do anything about it. He had contracted the rare muscle disease amyotrophic lateral sclerosis, a fatal illness now called, "Lou Gehrig's Disease." Two years later, Gehrig died just two weeks short of his 38th birthday.

Lou Gehrig being congratulated after his home run in game four of the 1937 World Series. It was his last postseason four-bagger. Gehrig had a .731 slugging percentage in World Series play. In 1939, when he called it quits, Gehrig was 4-for-28, all singles.

Lou Gehrig during his speech.

Gehrig's farewell address

When it was discovered in May 1939 that the New York Yankees captain and first baseman was dying of an incurable muscular disease, the team announced that Independence Day, July 4, would also be "Lou Gehrig Appreciation Day." With two generations of Bronx Bombers (including Babe Ruth and the rest of the 1927 "Murderer's Row" team) and nearly 62,000 fans present to honor "The Pride of the Yankees," Gehrig made the most emotional and memorable speech in baseball history.

"I may have been given a bad break," Gehrig told the crowd, "but I have an awful lot to live for. Today, I consider myself the luckiest man on the face of the earth."

The fans rose, almost as one, and rocked the stadium with chants of, "We love you, Lou."

BOB FELLER'S OPENING DAY NO-HITTER

The ultimate baseball phenomenon, Iowa-born Bob Feller was signed—in violation of baseball's rules—by the Cleveland Indians before he was graduated from high school. One look convinced them that he would be wasted in the minors, and Feller burst upon the major league scene in 1936 with a 15-strikeout, 4-1 win over the St. Louis Browns. Two years later, he set a new record for game strikeouts with 18 and led the American League in strikeouts for the first time with 240. By this time, Feller's blazing fastball was legendary. Many were calling it the fastest of all time. In a famous filmed stunt, Feller's fastball raced and beat a motorcycle doing 95 mph.

The next stop on Feller's dizzying upward course was a league-high 24 wins in 1939; he also led the AL in games, shutouts, innings pitched, strikeouts (again), and ERA. Practically the only pitching feat to elude Feller up to that point was a no-hitter. Not that he hadn't come close; three near misses—one in 1938, two in '39, each spoiled by a bunt or scratch hit—had put the baseball world on notice that it wouldn't have to wait much longer.

Not a day longer, as it turned out. On the first day of the 1940 season, April 16, Feller no-hit the Chicago White Sox 1-0. Although he walked five, he won the game easily. The lone White Sox rally began when three walks loaded the bases with two out in the second and ended when Bob Kennedy struck out. The game's only other dramatic moment came with two down in the ninth, when shortstop Luke Appling, a .310 lifetime hitter, clouted one 3-2 pitch after another deep to right field in foul territory. After the fourth time, Feller gave in and threw ball four, as he later conceded, intentionally. Second baseman Ray Mack ended the game when he dove for Taffy Wright's smash toward right, knocked it down then picked it up, and threw him out by a step. It was the first Opening Day no-hitter in American League history and the first in the majors since Giants hurler Red Ames lost on Opening Day, 1909, after pitching 10 no-hit frames.

The 1940 season ended very differently for Feller than it began. He lost the pennant-clincher to Detroit on the next-to-last day of the season despite allowing only three hits and two runs. He came back with another great season in 1941, winning 25 games and fanning 260. World War II then engaged Feller until late 1945, giving his right arm, which had endured 663 innings, a break. Feller returned from the service to win 20 games three more times in nine full seasons and finish with a record of 266-162, including three no-hitters and a record dozen one-hit games.

Bob Feller on opening day, 1940. In addition to his three no-hitters, he hurled a record 12 one-hitters, of which seven could have been hitless but for fluke singles or controversial scorer's decisions. Had his career not been interrupted by a Navy hitch, Feller probably would have had more wins than all but four pitchers in this century.

Floyd Giebell

Floyd Giebell beats Bob Feller to clinch AL pennant

The 1940 AL race was a clogged battle between the Indians, Tigers, and Yankees. Led by 21-year-old ace Bob Feller, who won 27 games, the Indians were three games behind the Tigers going into a season-ending three-game series with Detroit. Needing only one win to clinch, Tigers manager Del Baker saved his top pitchers for the final two games and threw a journeyman named Floyd Giebell (who had pitched only twice that season) against Feller, practically conceding a loss. But the gamble paid off. One two-run Rudy York homer turned out to be enough against Feller as Giebell pitched the game of his life. Every hard-hit ball by Cleveland landed in a Detroit glove. The Tigers prevailed 2-0 to win the pennant. Feller went on to win almost 200 more games lifetime; Giebell never won another game in the majors.

JOE DiMAGGIO HITS SAFELY IN 56 CONSECUTIVE GAMES

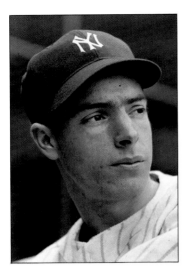

To those who saw him play, Joe DiMaggio had a mystical grace about him that transcended his statistics, great as they were. It is perhaps fitting then that he had a predilection for streaks. Most who know about DiMaggio's major league record 56-game hitting streak in 1941 don't know that, immediately afterward, he started in on a 16-game streak; even fewer are aware that when he was 18 and playing in the Pacific Coast League, he put together a 61-game streak.

It wasn't news when Joe started his streak with a scratch single off Edgar Smith of the White Sox on May 15. Things got interesting around game 30, when the newspapers began to dust off old hitting streak marks, like George McQuinn's 34-game streak, which DiMaggio equaled on June 21. By the time he surpassed Ty Cobb's 1911 40-game streak and George Sisler's 1922 American League record 41, the "Yankee Clipper" was a national sensation. Pressure was building not only on Joe but on official scorers, opposing fielders, and especially pitchers, who wanted to end the streak but not to cheat posterity by pitching around him. On July 2, DiMaggio homered off Boston's Dick Newsome to move past the major league record of 44 games set by Baltimore's Wee Willie Keeler back in 1897 (before foul balls counted as strikes).

Two weeks later, 67,468 Cleveland fans saw the streak come to an end. Twice, third baseman Ken Keltner made sparkling plays on DiMaggio drives down the line. In the eighth inning, DiMaggio hit a hard grounder up the middle that appeared to take a sudden hop toward the glove of shortstop Lou Boudreau, who started a 6-4-3 double play.

Looking at the statistical summary, DiMaggio's streak becomes even more miraculous. Overall, he batted .408 (relatively low considering that he had to distribute only 91 hits over the 56 games). He made four hits in a game only four times and 34 times kept the streak alive with a single hit. On several occasions the streak hung by the slenderest of threads—many of them, curiously, coming against the White Sox. In games 30 and 31, DiMaggio got bad-hop singles off the body of White Sox shortstop Luke Appling; in number 54, his only hit was a dribbler that Chicago third baseman Bob Kennedy couldn't handle. Facing his great pitching nemesis Sox righty Johnny Rigney four times during the streak, DiMaggio barely managed to squeak by, going 1-3, 1-5, 1-4, and 1-3 for a .267 average.

DiMaggio's streak carried the Yankees from a .500 record to first place by a good margin. Far from shortening his swing for the sake of a record, Joe produced runs in abundance; in 223 at-bats, he scored 56 runs, drove in 55, and hit half of his season total of 30 homers. This, and not the streak, is why DiMaggio was voted MVP over the .406-hitting Ted Williams.

Joe DiMaggio excelled in all phases of the game, but he was often hurt. He played in only 139 games in 1941 due to an ankle injury that forced him to sit out much of August, but he still led the AL with 125 RBI. DiMaggio struck out but 13 times in '41 and had 76 bases on balls.

Ken Keltner

Ken Keltner is remembered primarily in association with the great DiMaggio Streak. He was, however, one of the better third basemen of his day, playing 11 seasons with the Indians and batting .276 lifetime. The two magnificent stops he made on DiMaggio were no aberration; he regularly led the league at his position in assists, fielding, and double plays—turning it 37 times in 1944, 38 in 1942, and 40 in 1939.

Keltner could hit, too, producing around 30 doubles, nine triples, and 20 homers in an average season, and driving in more than 110 runs twice. He once again rose to the occasion in '48, batting .297 with 91 runs, 31 homers, and 119 RBI to propel Cleveland to an AL pennant and the World Championship.

Joe DiMaggio broke Wee Willie Keeler's record of 44 straight games on July 2. That day Joltin' Joe belted his 15th home run during the streak.

Joe DiMaggio hits safely in his 43rd consecutive game on July 1 against Boston (opposite page, top). He got two hits in that contest, the first off starter Mickey Harris and the second off Mike Ryba. Phil Rizzuto, then a 22-year-old rookie, with his hand on DiMaggio's shoulder (opposite page, bottom) as the two watch batting practice prior to a 1941 game. In his last at-bat on the night his 56-game streak ended, DiMaggio smacked a ball that he deemed one of the hardest shots he ever hit; Indians shortstop Lou Boudreau (this page) turned it into a routine double play.

TED WILLIAMS IS LAST TO BETTER .400 BARRIER BY BATTING .406

Ted Williams and Joe DiMaggio were two of the greatest hitters in history. Both contemporaries and rivals, the Red Sox slugger and the Yankees center fielder were as different from each other as two players could be. No season illustrates this better than 1941, when both performed marvels, since unequaled, with different results. DiMaggio had "The Streak," batted .357, and helped the Yankees take the pennant. Williams was the last batter to hit over .400, led DiMaggio in on-base average .551 to .440 and in slugging .735 to .643, and finished second by 17 games.

Williams was a lifetime .344 hitter who won the Triple Crown in 1942 and '47 (three Triple Crowns in seven years, if his minor league feat with the Minneapolis Millers of the American Association is counted). He hit over .320 in 12 of 13 full seasons and won seven batting titles. Williams was a good candidate to bat .400, primarily because of his terrific strike-zone judgment. His batting eye may have been the best of all time; 11 times he drew more than 100 walks in a season and three times he drew more than 160. Besides the fact that this put opposing pitchers under pressure to throw strikes, Williams's ability to draw bases on balls meant that in his full seasons he averaged only 490 at-bats—and it's a lot easier to bat .400 in 500 at-bats than it is in 600.

As Williams freely admitted, there were a few additional factors working in his favor in 1941. The first was Fenway Park, which helped him so much throughout his career that DiMaggio, who played in an extreme pitchers' park, actually outhit Williams on the road (.333 lifetime to .328). Another was a minor leg injury that reduced his at-bats further, to 456, and spared him two weeks of playing in the cold, windy Boston April weather. Williams later told the story of how an obscure pitcher named Joe "Burrhead" Dobson helped him hone his skills during that time by playing daily simulated games. Dobson liked to bear down hard and use his whole pitching repertoire, giving Williams what he called "the most batting practice of my life, and the best."

All this, combined with the "good luck" presence of Red Sox coach Hugh Duffy (who in 1894 hit for the highest batting average in major league history, .440), helped Williams reach as high as .436 in June. He then began a long, steady slide, going down to .413 in September, then falling to .3995 with a doubleheader against Philadelphia left to play on the last day of the season (by contemporary baseball rules, this would round out to an official .400). Red Sox manager Joe Cronin urged him to sit the games out; Williams refused. That day, Williams went 6-8 with a home run to hit .406 the hard way.

Ted Williams connects as usual (top). Williams fanned just 27 times in 1941 and is one of only two sluggers (Mel Ott is the other) who hit more than 500 career homers while striking out fewer than 1,000 times. The Splendid Splinter being given batting tips by Hugh Duffy (bottom). In 1894, Duffy hit an all-time record .440.

Teddy Ballgame's All-Star blast

Joe DiMaggio outdid Ted Williams in the standings and in the MVP voting in 1941, but when their paths crossed in the All-Star Game on July 8 in Detroit, Williams outshone his Yankee rival. The American League was down 5-4 in the ninth after a pair of two-run homers from Pirates shortstop Arky Vaughn. With two outs, Williams came to bat against Cubs righty Claude Passeau and turned around a 2-1 fastball, sending it into the upper deck in right to win the game 7-5. Coming at a time when interleague rivalry excited great interest, this was one of the most dramatic and emotional All-Star victories ever.

MICKEY OWEN'S PASSED BALL FOILS BUMS

Joe DiMaggio's 56-game hitting streak and Ted Williams's .406 batting average may have been the top individual baseball stories of 1941, but the best team story of the year was the Brooklyn Dodgers. The fabled "Bums" won the National League pennant for the first time in 21 years.

Brooklyn General Manager Larry MacPhail was the architect of that Dodgers team, trading for players like second baseman Billy Herman from the Chicago Cubs and outfielder Joe Medwick from the St. Louis Cardinals. Another player MacPhail grabbed from the Cards was catcher Mickey Owen, who would figure prominently in one of the most memorable strike-outs in World Series history.

The 1941 Series between the Dodgers and the New York Yankees would be the first of many between the crosstown rivals, and the Yankees were heavily favored for this one. But the Bums played hard under 35-year-old manager Leo Durocher, winning game two 3-2 and losing games one and three by one run each, 3-2 and 2-1.

Game four was a must-win for Brooklyn, but they fell behind 3-2 after four innings. In the top of the fifth, the Yankees loaded the bases with two out, but the Dodgers colorful reliever Hugh Casey stopped the threat. Casey then pitched three scoreless innings while his team went ahead, 4-3.

In the top of the ninth, Casey retired the first two batters. He then went to a 3-2 count on Tommy Henrich. The next pitch (which some claimed was a spitball) sank out of the strike zone, but Henrich couldn't stop his swing and the game appeared to be over. But as Dodger fans cheered and Casey began walking off the mound in triumph, catcher Mickey Owen was racing for the ball, which had hit his mitt and bounced in foul ground behind the plate. Henrich instinctively ran for first base. The inning, and the Yanks, were still alive, but almost 34,000 Dodgers fans went silent, fearful that the mighty Bronx Bombers would take advantage of the miscue.

Sure enough, against a tiring Casey, DiMaggio followed with a single, Charlie Keller doubled in two runs, Bill Dickey walked, and Joe Gordon doubled in two more runs, putting the Yankees ahead, 7-4. The Dodgers would go down quietly in the ninth, and then in game five 3-1. Thus began a new tradition that would last until 1955: the Dodgers losing the World Series to the Yankees and Brooklyn fans crying, "Wait 'Til Next Year."

A dropped strike-three pitch turned a fine catcher into one of the game's all-time goats. As the *New York Times* wrote the day after the fateful fourth game, Mickey Owen's passed ball "doubtless will live through the ages of baseball like the Snodgrass muff and the Merkle [boner]."

Top: *Tommy Henrich breaking for first base as he realizes that Hugh Casey's third-strike pitch has eluded Dodgers catcher Mickey Owen. Henrich* (bottom) *was a native of Massilon, Ohio, and originally the property of the Indians. He became one of the Tribe's main nemeses after Judge Kenesaw Mountain Landis declared him a free agent.*

Hugh Casey

When Hugh Casey was converted from a starting pitcher to a reliever during the 1940 season, he became a predecessor to baseball's tradition of flaky relievers. Casey was an intense hurler; an animated character on the mound and a heavy drinker off it. In fact, Casey was a friend of the great American novelist Ernest Hemingway, and the two would engage in macho imbibing contests and fist-fights.

After winning 40 games primarily as a starter for the Dodgers from 1939 to 1941, Casey led the NL in saves in 1942 and '47. "Winding up in an exaggerated manner, like a rusty water pump," it was once written, "Casey would first go down to his knees and then up, throwing with manifest gusto."

CARDINALS DETHRONE YANKEES IN SERIES

Stan Musial

The New York Yankees were on a roll when it came to World Series play. Since losing to the St. Louis Cardinals in the 1926 fall classic, the Bronx Bombers had won all eight of their Series appearances, five in the previous six years. Now, 16 years later, they again were playing the Cardinals. The Yankees, not yet depleted by World War II summons, boasted such veterans as Joe DiMaggio, Bill Dickey, Charlie Keller, Joe Gordon, Phil Rizzuto, and Red Ruffing. The Cardinals, no longer the "Gas House Gang," were more like "Our Gang," stocked by general manager Branch Rickey with a bunch of young talent, led by 21-year-old rookie Stan Musial.

The Yanks established their dominance in the first game at St. Louis, scoring five runs in the last two innings for a 7-0 lead. The Cardinals scrapped for four runs against Ruffing and proved they would not be intimidated by the AL champions. The Yankees should have realized they'd have a battle on their hands, since St. Louis had gone 43-8 in its last 51 games (winning 106 overall) to overtake the 10-game lead the Brooklyn Dodgers had owned in early August.

In game two, St. Louis' 21-game winner, Johnny Beazley, pitched shutout ball for seven innings, until the Yankees tied the game 3-3 in the eighth. Musial drove in the winning run with a single in the ninth, and outfielder Enos Slaughter nailed a runner at third with nobody out to save the game. The Cardinals got great pitching and defense again in game three. While Terry Moore was robbing DiMaggio of extra bases with a diving catch in the sixth inning—and both Musial and Slaughter were making leaping catches near the bleachers in the seventh—lefty Ernie White was pitching a six-hit shutout. The Cards won 3-0.

Game four was a slugfest in which the teams were tied 6-6 going into the seventh, when the Cardinals broke through for two runs. Reliever Max Lanier then shut down the Yankees for the final three innings. It was Beazley versus Ruffing in game five. Rizzuto, who'd hit only seven homers in his first two seasons, belted a first-inning pitch into the left field seats to put the Yanks on top. Both teams scored single runs in the fourth before St. Louis went up by a run in the sixth. Then Beazley turned the Bombers into pop guns the rest of the game, and got some insurance when Whitey Kurowski hit a two-run homer. Any chance the Yankees had to tie it in the ninth was snuffed out when Joe Gordon was picked off second with none out.

The Cardinals batted just .239 for the Series, but won in five games with great pitching and stellar defense.

Top: *Cardinal third baseman Whitey Kurowski catches Joe Gordon's pop foul as Marty Marion drops to the ground in the 1942 Series. The Cardinals mob Johnny Beazley* (bottom) *after the finale. Beazley came from nowhere to win 21 games in '42 and two more in the Series. Returning from the armed services in 1946, he won just nine more games.*

ST. LOUIS BROWNS WIN FIRST PENNANT

Vern Stephens

The St. Louis teams in both the NL and AL were the last original franchises to win a pennant. It took 51 years, but such talents as Rogers Hornsby and Jim Bottomley finally brought National League pennant-winning-caliber play to the Cardinals in 1926. Rather than improving their club, the St. Louis Browns waited for World War II and the military draft to bring the rest of the American League down to their level.

The Brownies epitomized the ragged state of wartime baseball. They had nine players age 34 or older and history's first-ever all-4F infield.

The Browns had a dismal history prior to 1944. The franchise bottomed out in 1939, when the team lost 111 games and came in 64^1/$_2$ games in back of New York. In the years between 1940 and 1943, they averaged 25 games out and fifth place in the standings. Even counting the pennant season of 1944, they drew a total of just 3,330,861 fans for the entire decade; in 1941, fewer than 200,000 fans saw the Browns play. They weren't much better after 1944, finishing sixth or seventh seven times before giving up and moving to Baltimore for the 1954 season.

But in 1944, St. Louis had its moment of glory. Led by 23-year-old slugging shortstop Vern Stephens (who hit .293 with 20 home runs and a league-high 109 RBI), .295-hitting Milt Byrnes, and Mike Kreevich (the only member of the team to bat over .300—at .301), the Browns offense scored a respectable 684 runs. Their pitching was solid as well. Old Nels Potter and young Jack Kramer won 19 and 17 games, respectively; the staff was rounded out by Bob Muncrief, Denny Galehouse, and the 34-year-old Sig Jackucki. Jackucki was a classic product of a time when teams had to advertise for ballplayers in the help-wanted sections of newspapers. An 0-3 lifetime pitcher who had retired in 1939, Jackucki was re-discovered in a Houston factory league and given a spot in the Browns' rotation. He went 13-9 with a 3.55 ERA.

Jackucki's 13th victory gave St. Louis the pennant after a tense, three-team September dogfight. On September 29, St. Louis knocked the New York Yankees out of contention with a doubleheader sweep, followed by another win the next day. The Detroit Tigers won two of three from Washington to drop into a tie for first place with the Browns. Then, on the final day of the season, the Tigers 27-game winner and AL ERA-leader Dizzy Trout lost to the Senators while two homers by Chet Laabs and one by Vern Stephens gave the Browns the victory over New York and clinched the pennant, by one game, over Detroit. The Brownies' .578 winning percentage tied a then record for the lowest by a pennant-winner—set in 1926 by the Cardinals.

George McQuinn (top) is greeted by Browns teammates Mark Christman (6) and Gene Moore (15) after hitting his game-winning two-run homer in the Series opener. Bottom: The Browns celebrate the club's only pennant. Sig Jakucki, who won the crucial game, is the bare-chested oldster in the foreground with his arms around Vern Stephens* (left) *and Chet Laabs* (right).

Luke Sewell

All-St. Louis World Series

The Cardinals won their third-straight National League pennant to make the 1944 World Series a one-city affair. It was baseball's only all-St. Louis Series. It was a homey event: The Browns were the Cardinals' landlords at Sportsman's Park. Managers Billy Southworth (Cards) and Luke Sewell (Browns), accustomed to one team always being on the road, found their shared apartment suddenly cramped.

The Cardinals took the six-game Series in six days, but the underdog Browns put up a fight. They outpitched the Cardinals but were let down by their hitting and fielding. Don Gutteridge and Vern Stephens made three errors apiece and the Browns committed 10 to the Cards' one.

HANK GREENBERG'S GRAND SLAM WINS PENNANT

By late summer of 1945, the American League race looked like a near repeat of 1944, with Washington, New York, St. Louis, and Detroit all in the hunt. That year, however, former major leaguers began to return from military service. The returnee with the biggest impact on the season was slugger Hank Greenberg, who came in to pick up a Tigers team that was barely holding on, thanks to the pitching of Hal Newhouser (who went 25-9 with a 1.81 ERA and won the MVP Award).

It wasn't the first time that Greenberg's heroics had made the difference for the Tigers. In 1934, he batted .339 with 63 doubles as Detroit won the pennant. The next year, he had 36 homers, 170 RBI, a .328 average, and was voted the unanimous MVP; Detroit won again. After losing 1936 to injury, the big first baseman in 1937 upped his home run total to 40, hit .337, and knocked in 183 runs—the third-highest RBI count in history. In '38, he scored and drove in a combined 290 runs while confronting Babe Ruth's homer record, falling two short at 58. In 1940, Greenberg won the MVP for the second time as his 50 doubles, 41 homers, and 150 RBI paced Detroit to another pennant. Even in his "off" season of 1939, he hit .312 with 33 home runs and 112 RBI.

One of the first big-leaguers to enter the service, Greenberg left Detroit 19 games into the 1941 campaign, not to return until July 1, 1945. He homered in his first game back against Philadelphia and then began to play himself back into shape. By mid-September, Detroit had a one and one-half game lead after taking three of five from second-place Washington and their all-knuckleballing pitching staff.

As in 1944, the pennant race came down to a crucial series between Detroit and St. Louis; the Senators would gain a tie if the Browns could manage a doubleheader sweep on the final day of the season. Virgil Trucks started for Detroit in game one against the 15-11 Nels Potter for St. Louis. With the Tigers up 2-1, Newhouser relieved Trucks in the sixth inning and narrowly escaped a bases-loaded, one-out situation. In the seventh, though, he allowed Gene Moore and Pete Gray to score the tying and go-ahead runs. The score remained 3-2 in the ninth, when leadoff man Hub Walker, pinch-hitting for Newhouser, walked and Skeeter Webb bunted his way on. After another bunt moved both runners into scoring position, Potter walked Doc Cramer to load the bases and go for the double-play with Greenberg. Greenberg clouted his 11th career grand slam to win the game and another pennant for Detroit. In 270 at-bats, less than a half-season, the 34-year-old Greenberg had scored 47 runs and driven in 60 on 35 extra-base hits to finish with a .311 batting average.

Hank Greenberg batting, shortly after his return to the game in 1945. His best days behind him, he still led the AL in homers and RBI the following year, but in doing so became the first in history to hit 40 or more homers while batting under .300. He smashed 331 career home runs despite playing more than 75 games in only 10 seasons.

Pete Gray

Pete Gray played 77 games for the 1945 Browns, batting .218 with six doubles and two triples, to become one of the most celebrated handicapped players ever.

Despite his poor 1945 record, Gray was not a publicity stunt. Lacking most of his right arm, he batted .333 and stole 68 bases to become MVP of the Southern Association in 1944. His undoing was big league off-speed pitching—the undoing of many other ballplayers. There have been other legitimate handicapped major leaguers. Hugh "One-Arm" Daily won 73 games, including a no-hitter. The most successful of them all—Mordecai "Three-Finger" Brown, who compiled a 2.06 ERA over 14 seasons—attributed the unpredictable break of his famous curveball to his deformed hand.

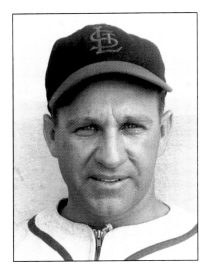

ENOS SLAUGHTER'S DASH HOME WINS SERIES

Stan Musial and Ted Williams returned home from the war in 1946 to lead their respective teams to pennants. Musial batted .365 with 50 doubles and 124 runs scored. Williams hit .342 with 38 homers, as Boston finished 12 games up. Both were MVPs.

As has happened so many times in postseason history, the big guys bombed in the 1946 World Series—Musial hit .222 and Williams hit .200—and vacated center stage in favor of such little guys as Rudy York, Harry Brecheen, and Enos "Country" Slaughter. Even rookie catcher Joe Garagiola had a four-hit game.

In the second-most dramatic game of the seven-game Series, York's 10th-inning home run beat the Cardinals' 21-game winner Howie Pollet 3-2 in game one. The next day, Brecheen, the lefty who had gone only 15-15 on the season, shut down Boston on four hits to win 3-0 and even up the Series. Boston ace Boo Ferriss then unevened it 4-0 with an equally masterful six-hitter; York contributed a three-run homer off loser Murry Dickson. The two teams traded victories again in games four and five. St. Louis brought back Brecheen for game six; his second Series win, by a 4-1 score, tied things up once again, and set up a Dickson-Ferriss confrontation to decide the championship.

The score was 3-1 Cardinals after seven; Dickson had held Boston to three hits—and had doubled in the second run and scored the third. Then, in the top of the eighth, Red Sox Rip Russell singled and George Metkovich doubled to put the tying runs in scoring position with none out. Dyer signaled to the bullpen for Brecheen to pitch to lefthanders Wally Moses and Johnny Pesky, only one day after having gone nine innings. Moses struck out and Pesky lined out, but righty Dom DiMaggio doubled both runs in to tie the game at 3-3. The two-out pop-up by Williams let the go-ahead run die on second.

In the Cardinal half of the eighth, Slaughter singled to lead off. Two quick outs later, lefthanded slap-hitter Harry Walker followed with a liner over shortstop into left-center field and, somehow, Slaughter scored from first base. Brecheen got his third win and St. Louis won the Series 4-3. This play is still being debated today: Did shortstop Pesky hesitate before relaying the center fielder's throw home? Was it the fault of second baseman Bobby Doerr or third baseman Mike Higgins for not warning Pesky? Should Walker's hit have been scored a single instead of a double? Or did Boston do everything more or less right, but Slaughter, with two outs and World Series money on the line, simply ran three base-lengths faster than two men could throw a baseball roughly the same distance?

Enos Slaughter successfully stealing home in the 1946 World Series (top). *He stole just nine bases that year, a personal high, but was always a threat to go when the game was on the line.* Bottom: *Though it was still early in the careers of both Ted Williams and Stan Musial, neither of the era's top two players ever appeared in another Series after 1946.*

Harry Brecheen

Cardinals win first ever NL playoff

The 1946 pennant race was a season-long duel between the Branch Rickey-led Brooklyn Dodgers and the Rickey-built St. Louis Cardinals. St. Louis dropped as far as seven and one-half games back on July 2. The Dodgers, nevertheless, after a slow fade, backed into a season-ending tie with the Cardinals (both teams lost their season finales). The deadlock necessitated the first pennant playoff by a never-before-used NL rule, a best-before-used NL rule, a best two-out-of-three series.

Dodgers manager Leo Durocher won a coin toss and chose to play game one in St. Louis, thereby guaranteeing home-field advantage in games two and three. His strategy backfired as Howie Pollett threw a complete-game 4-2 victory over Ralph Branca. St. Louis in game two brought an 8-1 lead into the ninth before Brooklyn staged a desperate, ninth-inning rally that plated three runs. Harry Brecheen then came on in relief with the bases loaded and struck out Howie Schultz, the potential tying run.

JACKIE ROBINSON BREAKS BASEBALL'S COLOR BARRIER

There are two ways of looking at Jackie Robinson's breaking of baseball's color line in 1947. One view is that World War II probably spelled the beginning of the end for many forms of institutionalized racism in America. Another perspective is that baseball's integration came about primarily through Dodger executive Branch Rickey's clever manipulation of events and Robinson's personal courage. Either way, the integration experiment succeeded for one reason: Jackie Robinson was a winning ballplayer.

Baseball's color line began in 1884, when brothers Moses and Welday Walker of the American Association became the last blacks allowed to play in the majors for 61 years. In 1945, Rickey decided the time was right for the next black big-leaguer. He wanted a man who was comfortable in the white world, educated, and self-disciplined enough not to respond to the hostility that he would inevitably encounter—in short, someone acceptable to mainstream whites. As a 28-year-old former Army officer and UCLA football star with a bland California accent, Robinson fit the bill and Rickey signed him to a Triple-A contract with the Montreal Royals for the 1946 season.

Even Robinson's former Negro League teammates were surprised at how well he played in Montreal. Robinson hit .349 with a league-leading 113 runs scored and was the International League Rookie of the Year. It was Rickey's turn to be surprised when the Dodgers players nevertheless refused to accept him in spring training of 1947. Things came to a head when a group of Dodgers—not, contrary to popular belief, exclusively Southerners—got up an anti-Robinson petition. After Rickey threatened to trade the petitioners and Dodger manager Leo Durocher personally confronted them, most of them backed down and Robinson opened the season as the Dodgers first baseman. Although the feelings of his teammates mellowed to mere indifference and the Brooklyn fans welcomed him, opposing teams and their fans tortured Robinson in the opening weeks of the '47 season with the vilest possible insults as well as knockdown pitches and intentional spikings. Robinson stoically played his hardest, and by the end of the year he had a league-leading 29 stolen bases, 125 runs scored, the NL Rookie of the Year Award—and an ulcer. The Dodgers had a pennant.

By 1949, Robinson had moved to second base, his natural position. Now a team leader on and off the field, he helped Brooklyn to his second of six pennants with an MVP season that included a batting title, 122 runs scored, 124 RBI, 37 stolen bases, and 16 home runs. He had five more solid seasons, retiring with a .311 career batting average. He left behind a legacy of excellence in nearly every area of the game and courage on and off the field.

Jackie Robinson slides safely into third base (top) as Braves third sacker Bob Elliott takes the throw. Branch Rickey carefully watches Robinson put his signature to his historic first contract in Organized Baseball (bottom). Rickey picked Robinson to break the color line because he knew that Robinson would have the courage "not to fight back."

Larry Doby

Larry Doby was the first black man to play in the American League and the second in the majors. He had to show as much tolerance and valor as did Jackie Robinson. A second baseman by trade, Doby came up in late '47 and was converted to a center fielder for the 1948 season. He batted .301 that year, displaying both power and an apt batting eye. To the dismay of anti-integrationists, the Indians won the pennant just as Robinson's Dodgers had done the year before. Now just another winning ballplayer, Doby went on to score or drive in 100 runs in a season eight times. In 1952, he hit 32 homers to become the first black player to lead either league, then repeated this feat in Cleveland's 111-win, pennant-winning 1954 campaign.

Jackie Robinson was
a great all-around
athlete who had 11
yards a carry one
year at UCLA in
football and led
the Pacific Coast
Conference in scoring
twice in basketball.

Jackie Robinson (opposite page, top), a second baseman with his first team in Organized Baseball, the 1946 Montreal Royals, led the International League with a .346 batting average that year. Opposite page, bottom: Robinson was a running back at UCLA. Another college star of Robinson's era, Kenny Washington, was the first black to play in the modern National Football League. Robinson snares a high line drive (this page).

COOKIE LAVAGETTO AND AL GIONFRIDDO BLAZE IN LOSING SERIES

Al Gionfriddo

It had been six years since the crosstown rival New York Yankees and Brooklyn Dodgers had met in the World Series, so the cast of characters on both sides was vastly different from the teams that faced each other in the 1941 Series. Oh, Joe DiMaggio was still around, but the two most prominent new faces were Dodgers rookie second baseman Jackie Robinson and Yankees rookie catcher Yogi Berra. The most memorable moments of the 1947 Series (besides the fact that it was the first fall classic to be televised), however, were not supplied by the high-profile rookies, but by two Dodgers who weren't exactly household names in New York.

The Yankees were leading the Series two games to one going into the pivotal game four at Ebbets Field. The Bronx Bombers starter was Bill Bevens, who was a dreary 7-13 on the season. Bevens was wild but fast on this day, and though he was walking batters all afternoon (he set a Series record with 10), he constantly escaped trouble. By the bottom of the ninth, the Yanks were leading 2-1 (great relief pitching by Hugh Casey had kept the game close) and Bevens was pitching a no-hitter.

Two outs away from immortality, Bevens walked Carl Furillo. After pinch-runner Al Gionfriddo stole second, Pete Reiser was intentionally walked. This was a controversial decision by Yankees manager Bucky Harris, since it's a baseball sin to put the winning run on base. Cookie Lavagetto, batting for Eddie Stanky, blasted Bevens's second pitch off the right field wall for a double, breaking up the no-hitter and winning the game for the Dodgers 3-2.

The Yankees rebounded to win game five 2-1. The Dodgers needed two wins at Yankee Stadium. A crowd of 74,065 watched as the Dodgers went ahead in game six 4-0, then trailed 5-4, then took the lead again with four runs in the sixth, 8-5. In the bottom of the sixth, the Yankees put two runners on with two out before DiMaggio stepped up. On lefthander Joe Hatten's first pitch, DiMaggio sent a fly ball to deep left field that looked like a game-tying homer. But Gionfriddo, inserted for defense that inning, raced to the 415 mark, leaped backward, and caught the ball in the webbing of his glove just before hitting the fence. In a rare display of emotion, DiMaggio kicked the dirt at second base. Dodgers announcer Red Barber later told Gionfriddo he'd made "an impossible catch."

Unfortunately, Lavagetto's and Gionfriddo's heroics didn't help Brooklyn win the Series, as the Yankees took game seven 5-2. It didn't even help the two sudden stars keep their jobs. After the '47 Series, they (along with Bill Bevens) never played another game in the major leagues.

Cookie Lavagetto hits his pinch double (top) *that drives in Al Gionfriddo and Pete Reiser to win game four of the 1947 World Series. The hit broke up Bill Bevens's no-hitter.* Bottom: *Bedlam breaks loose as Lavagetto is greeted by his Dodger teammates after his heroics. It was his last major league hit.*

Red Barber's World Series calls

The memorable 1947 World Series was made even more historic by Hall of Fame announcer Red Barber, whose classic calls of Cookie Lavagetto's game four ninth-inning hit and Al Gionfriddo's game six catch are now a part of baseball broadcasting lore. The "Old Redhead" was on the top of his play-by-play game during the entire Series.

On Lavagetto's clout: "There's a drive into the left field corner. Back goes Henrich. He can't get it. It's off the wall for a base hit. Here comes the ... tying run ... and here comes ... the ... winning ... run!"

On Gionfriddo's grab: "Swung on—belted. It's a long one, deep into left center. Back goes Gionfriddo. Back ... back ... back .... He makes a one-handed catch against the bullpen. Ohhhh, Doctor!"

Cookie Lavagetto, Al Gionfriddo, and Bill Bevens are linked forever in baseball history for the '47 fall classic. After the Series, the three of them never played another major league game.

Al Gionfriddo spearing Joe DiMaggio's long drive just as it was about to clear the low bullpen barrier in deep left-center field in Yankee Stadium (opposite page), in the sixth inning of game six of the 1947 World Series. Bill Bevens lets one go in game six of the '47 fall classic (this page). Bevens was a 7-13 pitcher for the Yankees during the regular season that year.

CLEVELAND BEATS BOSTON
IN FIRST AL PLAYOFF

Joe Gordon

After getting his team up to fourth place in 1947, the Cleveland Indians' flamboyant owner, Bill Veeck, pulled out all the stops. He had signed Larry Doby (the AL's first black player) in 1947; added in 1948 such role players as Thurman Tucker, Allie Clark, and Russ Christopher; held promotional days for his players and the fans; and in July signed 42-year-old Negro League legend Satchel Paige. Satchel bolstered a pitching staff led by 19-game winner Bob Feller and 20-game winners Bob Lemon and rookie Gene Bearden. Such players as second baseman Joe Gordon (32 homers and 124 RBI), Doby (.301 average with 14 homers and 66 RBI), and third baseman Ken Keltner (31 homers and 119 RBI) provided the offense. It all worked for Veeck as the Indians drew more than 2.2 million fans and were in the middle of the American League's hottest pennant race in years.

The Indians had clinched a tie on the season's next to last day when Bearden beat the Tigers. Detroit's Hal Newhouser then beat Feller in the finale while the Boston Red Sox took the Yankees, leaving the Tribe and the BoSox with identical 96-58 records.

The first pennant playoff in AL history, a one-game affair, was billed as a hitting battle, mainly between Boston's Ted Williams (who batted a league-best .369) and Cleveland's 32-year-old shortstop/manager Lou Boudreau, who hit .355, scored 116 runs, drove in 106 runs, and won the AL Most Valuable Player Award. With the game at Boston's Fenway Park, Boudreau stacked his lineup with righthanded hitters to go after the huge but close "Green Monster" wall in left field. However, Boudreau shocked everyone by pitching the lefty Bearden rather than one of his righties. Still, any Indians starter would have been better than the 36-year-old journeyman the Sox were throwing named Denny Galehouse.

Boudreau, who had always hit well in Fenway, got the Indians rolling in the first inning with a homer over the 37-foot wall. Boston tied the score immediately in the bottom of the first, even though Boudreau—playing the lefty Williams up the middle—robbed the Splendid Splinter of a hit that could have led to a big inning. The game remained 1-1 until the fourth when both Boudreau and Gordon singled, and then Keltner hit a three-run blast over the Monster. When Boudreau conquered the wall again in the fifth, the score was 6-1, and it was all over for Boston. Bearden fed the Red Sox a steady diet of knuckleballs, held the great Williams to one hit on the day, and won 8-3. Cleveland went on to play another Boston team—the National League's Braves—in the World Series, which they won in six games.

Gene Bearden (without the cap) celebrates after beating the Red Sox in the playoff (top). Player/manager Lou Boudreau is in the center and coach Mel Harder is at right. Bottom: Bearden being carried off the field by jubilant teammates after he beat the Sox 8-3 in Fenway for the 1948 flag. It was Bearden's 20th win that season.

Satchel Paige debuts in
the major leagues

Leroy Robert "Satchel" Paige was a 42-year-old Negro League legend when Bill Veeck signed him to a major league contract on July 7, 1948. The baseball community was shocked, calling the signing "another Veeck publicity stunt." *The Sporting News*, then called "the Bible of Baseball," said that "bringing in a rookie of Paige's age is to demean the standards of baseball." But Satch proved he could still pitch. In his first two relief outings, he threw five scoreless innings, picking up one win. On August 13, in front of 51,000 fans at Comiskey Park, he started and shut out the White Sox. One week later in Cleveland, with over 78,000 in attendance, he blanked the ChiSox again, 1-0. Paige went 6-1 for the year and helped the Indians win a World Championship.

PHILLIE WHIZ KIDS CAPTURE PENNANT

Eddie Sawyer

The young 1950 Phillies, nicknamed the "Whiz Kids," are one of baseball's great Cinderella stories. After coming up 16 games short in 1949, the Phillies found that they had the NL's best pitching staff in 1950. Primarily responsible were a maturing Robin Roberts and Jim Konstanty, one of the early modern-style relief aces who appeared in a league-leading 74 games in relief. Konstanty won 16, saved 22, and was voted NL MVP. The Phils featured an above-average attack of Eddie Waitkus (102 runs), Richie Ashburn (.303 average), and Del Ennis (.311 average, 126 RBI). They also led the majors in colorful names, including Swish Nicholson, Granny Hamner, Puddin' Head Jones, and the immortal Putsy Caballero. On September 15, this group was steaming along, nine games ahead of second-place Brooklyn.

Then midnight struck. Philadelphia lost eight out of 10, including back-to-back doubleheader sweeps at the hands of the Giants, while the Dodgers were riding a seven-game winning streak. The Phillies' final two games were against Brooklyn at Ebbets Field. When the Dodgers took the first game 7-3, the Phillies had totaled seven blown games in the standings over a nine-day period. One more loss would mean that the season would end in a tie. The Phils came into the most important game of the season tired and hurting. With few other options, manager Eddie Sawyer called on Roberts to pitch his third start in five days.

Opposing Roberts was fellow staff ace and 19-game winner Don Newcombe. The two matched zeroes until the sixth, when the Phillies scored on Jones's RBI single. Dodger Pee Wee Reese tied it up with a homer. There was no more action until the bottom of the ninth, when Cal Abrams drew a walk and Reese singled him to second. Next, Duke Snider singled to center, sending Abrams running for home. Center fielder Richie Ashburn had collected only seven assists on the season, but this time he fired a strike to catcher Andy Seminick that put Abrams out by what Red Smith called "12 fat feet." Roberts then intentionally walked Jackie Robinson, got Carl Furillo on a pop-up, and Gil Hodges on a fly.

In the top of the 10th, Roberts and Waitkus singled, but Ashburn uncharacteristically failed to bunt the runners over. Stepping up to the plate was outfielder Dick Sisler. A .276 lifetime hitter, he was an unlikely candidate for the hero's role (his father, though, was Hall of Famer George Sisler). Dick had singled three times off Newcombe that day, but his fourth hit was a high opposite-field drive that sliced into the left-field bleachers to win the game for Philadelphia, 4-1.

This was to be the Phillies' last win of 1950, however; they lost the World Series to the Yankees in four straight.

Finisher Jim Konstanty started the opener in the 1950 World Series (top) after he had been a reliever for 133 previous games for the Phillies. He is pitching to Gene Woodling, while Andy Seminick catches and Jocko Conlan umpires. Bottom: Joe DiMaggio slides safely into second while Mike Goliat waits for a throw from Granny Hamner in the '50 fall classic.

BOBBY THOMSON'S 'SHOT HEARD 'ROUND THE WORLD'

One of the most memorable moments in baseball history happened on October 1, 1951, when New York Giants outfielder Bobby Thomson hit a ninth-inning, three-run homer to beat the Brooklyn Dodgers and rip the collective heart out of fans of "Dem Bums."

It was the climax to a season known in baseball lore as "The Miracle of Coogan's Bluff," in which the Giants managed to overcome a 13½ game deficit with a little more than a month and a half left in the season. The Giants were in second place on August 12 when—with the help of a 20-year-old center fielder named Willie Mays—they reeled off 16 straight victories en route to a 37-7 record in their final 44 games. They caught the Dodgers two games from the finish line. Brooklyn had to come back from a 6-1 deficit in the season finale to beat the Phillies in 14 innings 9-8. Jackie Robinson hit the one-run shot, motoring Brooklyn to a tie record and forcing a three-game playoff between the archrival Giants and Dodgers.

Home runs by Monte Irvin and Thomson led the Giants to a 3-1 victory in game one. The Dodgers rebounded and blew the Giants away 10-0 in game two. For the deciding game at the Polo Grounds, Giants 23-game winner Sal Maglie faced Dodgers 20-game winner Don Newcombe. Brooklyn jumped ahead in the first inning on a Robinson single, and three runs in the eighth gave them a seemingly comfortable 4-1 lead.

But for these two teams, the ninth inning would become a microcosm of the entire season. With Newcombe tiring, Al Dark and Don Mueller singled. After Monte Irvin popped out, Whitey Lockman kept the rally going with a run-scoring double. With the tying runs in scoring position, Dodgers manager Charlie Dressen brought Ralph Branca in to pitch to Thomson, who wanted to redeem himself for an earlier base-running blunder and some bad fielding plays at third base that had contributed to Dodger runs.

Brooklyn could have walked Thomson, but that would have meant putting the winning run on base for the next batter, Willie Mays. Branca's first pitch to Thomson was a called strike. The next pitch was a fastball up and in, but Thomson hit it up and out of the park over the head of left fielder Andy Pafko. The ball landed just a few inches over the 315-mark. As Thomson circled the bases, suddenly a baseball immortal, radio broadcaster Russ Hodges screamed into his microphone: "The Giants win the pennant . . . ! The Giants win the pennant!" The Giant players and fans waited at home plate for their conquering hero.

To the Giants and the rest of baseball, Thomson's blast was "The Shot Heard 'Round the World."

A picture showing the path of Bobby Thomson's round-tripper, probably the most famous home run in baseball history. For Brooklyn, this homer was the embarrassing conclusion of a season in which the Dodgers had led the Giants by 13½ games on August 11.

Ralph Branca

After he served up that fateful home run pitch to Bobby Thomson in the final 1951 Dodgers-Giants playoff game, Ralph Branca walked dejectedly to the clubhouse, where he sat on the steps and cried. Branca has been remembered as the goat since, a shame because he was a pretty good pitcher.

From 1947 to 1951, Branca won 68 games for Brooklyn and lost just 47. Since he threw the gopher ball, Branca has been constantly reminded of his role in baseball's most memorable game, but he always handled it with grace and humor. "I look at it this way," he said. "Every time they mention Bobby Thomson's name, they mention my name, too. I'm just as immortal as he is."

BALLS OUTS TEAM INNING TEAM INNING
1 BKLYN 1 0 0 0 0 0 3 0
N.Y. 0 0 0 0 0 0 1 0

UMPIRES PLATE 6   1ST BASE 7   2ND BASE

Brooklyn left fielder Andy Pafko is a helpless witness (this page) *as Bobby Thomson's blast sails into the packed stands at the Polo Grounds. The Giants mob Thomson after his pennant-winning homer* (opposite page, top), *while dejected Dodgers pitcher Ralph Branca heads for the center field clubhouse* (opposite page, bottom). *Jackie Robinson (number 42) is watching to make absolutely sure that Thomson touches the plate before he surrenders to the inevitable.*

315 FT

Dodger manager
Chuck Dressen chose
to pitch to Bobby
Thomson, even
though first base
was open. The
on-deck batter was
Willie Mays.

JOE ADCOCK TOTALS 18 BASES IN ONE GAME

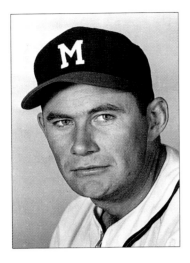

Hank Aaron, the man who would eventually become the all-time home run king, was a rookie for Milwaukee in 1954. The Braves counted on third baseman Eddie Mathews as their main power source. It was first baseman Joe Adcock, however, who provided the punch during a game in the middle of the '54 season.

The Braves had acquired Adcock in 1953 after he hit 31 homers over three seasons for the Cincinnati Reds. Ted Kluszweski was the Reds first baseman, so Adcock had to play in left field part-time to get his bat in the lineup. The powerfully built 6'4", 210-pounder provided his new team with a quick glimpse of his slugging potential when in April he became the first player to hit a ball over the 483-foot mark in center field at New York's Polo Grounds.

Adcock then put on an even more awesome hitting display on July 31, 1954, during a game against the Brooklyn Dodgers at Ebbets Field. Hitting fifth in a batting order that had Aaron third, Mathews fourth, and outfielder Andy Pafko sixth, Adcock homered his first time up against Don Newcombe. After smacking a double in his next at-bat, Adcock belted three homers his next three times at the plate—against three different pitchers: Erv Palica, Pete Wojey, and Johnny Podres. Adcock did all of this slugging with a borrowed piece of lumber.

"I broke my regular bat the night before," he said after his batting barrage. "So I borrowed one from [catcher] Charlie White. Boy, I could hardly lift it. It was the heaviest on the team."

Adcock put up some weighty numbers with that heavy bat, driving in seven runs with his four homers and one double. He set a major league record for total bases in a game that still stands, with 18. He scored five runs on his five at-bats. While 11 players have hit four homers in a game, none did it off four different hurlers. Mathews hit two home runs in the game and Pafko had one. Dodgers third baseman Don Hoak and first baseman Gil Hodges each added a homer, and the nine round-trippers resulted in a 15-7 Milwaukee win.

When Adcock hit a homer the next night, tying a record for home runs in consecutive games, pitchers finally fought back. Adcock was beaned by a fastball and was removed from the game on a stretcher. He didn't suffer long-term effects from the injury, but NL pitchers did. Adcock finished the season with 23 homers and would go on to blast 25 or more home runs five times in his career.

Joe Adcock scoring (top). He hit 336 career homers despite being platooned for several seasons during his prime, first in Cincinnati and then by Braves manager Fred Haney. Bottom: A radiant Adcock in the locker room after his record-shattering four home runs and 18 total bases in the Braves 15-7 win over the Dodgers on July 31, 1954.

WILLIE MAYS MAKES 'THE CATCH' IN WORLD SERIES

It's the top of the 10th inning, first game, 1954 World Series. The Cleveland Indians and New York Giants are tied 2-2. Vic Wertz leads off for the Tribe and lashes a shot up the left-center field gap at the Polo Grounds, around 440 feet away. The ball looks like it will go all the way to the wall for at least a triple, but Willie Mays, the Giants speedy and superb center fielder, backhands the ball, holding Wertz to a double. The Indians do not get the score, and the Giants eventually win the game in the bottom of the 10th 5-2.

New York wouldn't have even had a chance to win that game if not for a play Mays had made two innings earlier against Wertz—a play known simply as "The Catch."

The score was tied 2-2 in the top of the eighth with runners on first and second and none out. At the plate was Wertz, a fence buster who one season a few years earlier had 37 doubles and 27 homers. Lefthander Don Liddle was brought in for starter Sal Maglie to pitch to the lefthand-hitting Wertz. The strategy appeared to have backfired when Wertz sent Liddle's first delivery on a frozen rope to deep center field. Mays, though, got a great jump on what is the most difficult ball for a center fielder to handle. Racing full speed with his back to the plate, he came within 10 feet of the wall, stretched out his left arm, looked over his left shoulder, and stabbed the ball. He was nearly 460 feet from home plate. Then in one continuous motion, he pivoted toward the field, launched a perfect throw to the infield, and held baserunner Larry Doby from scoring from second base and Al Rosen from advancing from first. The Giants eventually got out of the inning unscathed. Many observers think that Mays's throw was as astonishing as his catch.

Right after the play, Giants radio announcer Russ Hodges said, "Willie Mays just made a catch that must have seemed like an optical illusion to a lot of folks." Dodgers general manager Branch Rickey sent Mays a note that read, "That was the finest catch I've ever seen, and the finest catch I ever hope to see." If Rickey did see similar catches over the next several years, they were probably made by Mays.

The "Say Hey Kid" wasn't through for the day. In the 10th inning, after making the second spectacular play (which Mays himself thought was a tougher play than The Catch), he walked, stole second, and scored the winning run on Monte Irvin's three-run homer. Inspired by Mays, the Giants went on to upset the favored Indians in a four-game sweep.

There may have been better defensive plays than Willie Mays's catch, but none has ever been more crucial. The Indians couldn't recover from it in the 1954 Series—and a case can be made that they still haven't. Mays's 2,843 career games rank second to Ty Cobb among outfielders, but Mays surpasses all with 7,095 putouts.

Bob Feller (left) *and Early Wynn*

Indians win 111 behind great pitching staff

The Cleveland Indians had been favored to win the 1954 World Series on the strength of their pitching staff, which led the team to one of the best records in baseball history—111-43. Bob Lemon, Early Wynn, and Mike Garcia went 23-7, 23-11, and 19-8, respectively, and each threw more than 250 innings.

Lemon and Wynn threw 41 complete games between them, and Garcia hurled five shutouts. Even 35-year-old Bob Feller contributed with a 13-3 record. The Indians posted an amazing 2.78 team ERA. Garcia, Lemon, and Wynn were the top three ERA pitchers in the league. It was the AL's best staff performance until the 1970 Orioles.

SANDY AMOROS'S CATCH REAPS SERIES FOR DODGERS

With rare exceptions, it was always the other guys and never the Brooklyn Dodgers who got the big hit or made the great play in postseason competition. Even when "Dem Bums" did special things, they couldn't convert them into championships. But finally, in 1955, the situation would change, thanks to left fielder Sandy Amoros.

It certainly didn't seem very different in the first two games of the Series against the Yankees, the fifth such matchup between the cross-town rivals (Brooklyn lost the previous four) since 1947. The Yankees, led by Yogi Berra, Mickey Mantle, Billy Martin, and manager Casey Stengel, took the games at Yankee Stadium, 6-5 and 4-2. No team had ever turned around a 2-0 deficit in the Series.

The Bums, though, bounced back in Brooklyn, winning all three games played at Ebbets Field, 8-3, 8-5, and 5-3. Amoros slugged a two-run homer in game five to help the Dodgers win. Whitey Ford's masterful four-hitter tied the Series at three, setting the stage for the Dodgers faithful to be heartbroken again.

A crowd of 63,000 watched young Brooklyn lefthander Johnny Podres (the game three winner) match zeros with Yankee Tommy Byrne for three innings. The Dodgers squeezed across single runs in the fourth and sixth for a 2-0 lead going into the bottom of the sixth. Dodger manager Walter Alston inserted Amoros as a defensive replacement in left field. It would prove to be the key strategic move of the Series. Amoros, a Cuban native, replaced Junior Gilliam, who in turn moved to second base replacing Don Zimmer.

With nobody out, Billy Martin walked and Gil McDougald beat out a bunt. Berra, Hank Bauer, and Moose Skowron were next up and Dodgers fans held their collective breath.

Brooklyn's outfield shifted towards right field for the lefthanded-hitting Berra, but Yogi crossed them up, hitting a long drive down the left field line. The blast looked like a sure hit, but Amoros raced toward the line, and at the last instant, reached out and speared the ball about knee high. It was fortunate for Amoros and the Dodgers that the outfielder was lefthanded so he didn't have to backhand the ball. Amoros abruptly stopped, whirled, and fired the ball to shortstop Pee Wee Reese, who in turn relayed to Gil Hodges, doubling McDougald off first base. McDougald, sure that the ball would drop (as was everyone else in Ebbets Field), had already passed second base before reversing his direction.

It would prove to be the last Yankees threat of the game as Podres allowed only three singles over the next three and one-third innings. Next year had finally arrived for the fans of Brooklyn.

Sandy Amoros snagging Berra's wrong-field drive. Left field was the Dodgers' Achilles' heel during the 1950s; Amoros did the job about as well as anyone prior to the arrival of Wally Moon in 1959. Brooklyn manager Walt Alston was a great believer in situational strategy, and this was a move that paid off handsomely.

Duke Snider

The Boys of Summer

Their names were Pee Wee, Jackie, and Campy. Gil, Duke, and Newk. Ersk, Shotgun, and The Preacher. They came close to the pinnacle of their profession every year for nearly ten seasons, but achieved it only once, in 1955. They were called "Dem Bums" by their fans and are now immortal-ized as "The Boys of Summer." Roger Kahn in 1971 wrote a best-selling book with that title, about his—a whole town's—love affair with the Brooklyn Dodgers, members of a family that included the fans who loved them—win or lose. By 1958, the team had moved to Los Angeles, ending a relationship between a team and its fans the likes of which baseball would never see again.

DON LARSEN TOSSES PERFECT GAME IN WORLD SERIES

What made the 1956 World Series different from the one played in 1955 was that the Yankees beat Brooklyn in seven. What made the two similar was that another relatively unknown player stole the spotlight and is now an immortal.

Going into the Series, 27-year-old Don Larsen was a lifetime 30-40 pitcher. In 1954, he had lost 21 games for the Orioles. In the second game of the '56 Series, he couldn't even make it past the second inning. But for one magical moment, Larsen—with good luck and outstanding fielding by his teammates—put it all together and pitched the only perfect game in Series history.

The Series was tied at two wins apiece when Larsen, an 11-7 pitcher on the season, started game five at Yankee Stadium. Employing an unusual no-windup delivery that he instituted late in the season, Larsen struck out two Dodgers in the first inning. One was Pee Wee Reese, whom he fanned on a 3-2 count. It would be the only time Larsen would throw three balls to a hitter in the entire game. In fact, in throwing just 97 pitches for the game, Larsen never hurled more than 15 pitches in any inning.

Dodgers hurler Sal "The Barber" Maglie matched Larsen out for out, retiring 11 Yankees in a row. The 12th batter, Mickey Mantle, homered in the fourth. When the Bombers picked up another run in the sixth, all eyes turned to Larsen.

Larsen's defense continually saved his perfecto with dazzling plays. In the second inning, Jackie Robinson hit a line drive off third baseman Andy Carey's glove, but shortstop Gil McDougald grabbed the ball in time to nail Robby. In the fifth inning, Gil Hodges hit a ball to deep left center that was turned into an out by Mantle's spectacular backhand catch. Sandy Amoros (the '55 Series hero) then hit a ball down the left field line that went foul by inches. In the seventh and eighth, McDougald and Carey both made excellent grabs of line drives.

By the top of the ninth, the crowd of 65,000 was cheering with every pitch Larsen threw. After the game, Larsen would say, "I was so weak in the knees out there in the ninth, I thought I was going to faint. My fingers didn't feel like they were on my hand."

Carl Furillo flied to right for the first out. Roy Campanella sent the first pitch deep to left that veered foul by inches before grounding out. Left-handed batter Dale Mitchell was sent up for Maglie. The first pitch was a ball. Then Larsen got a called strike and a swinging strike. Mitchell fouled off the next pitch before taking one on the corner that umpire Babe Pinelli called strike three. Yogi Berra ran out to Larsen and jumped into his arms.

Two views of Don Larsen hurling in his perfect game. Three days earlier the Dodgers had kayoed him in the second inning of game two and pinned a 13-8 loss on him. Like Yankee teammate Bullet Bob Turley, Larsen had switched to a no-windup delivery that seemed, for a short while at least, to make his delivery more effective.

Mickey Mantle

The 1950s Yankee Dynasty

There have been many great teams and even a few moderate dynasties in baseball history, but none compares with the New York Yankees teams of the '50s—if not in overall talent, then in ability to win titles. The Bronx Bombers won eight pennants during the decade (failing only in 1954 and 1959) and six World Championships (including the five in a row from 1949 to 1953). Over that glorious era, the Yankee roster was filled with such superstars as Joe DiMaggio, Yogi Berra, Phil Rizzuto, Mickey Mantle, Billy Martin, Elston Howard, Whitey Ford, and Allie Reynolds. They might not have been as formidable as the 1927 Yankees "Murderer's Row," but guided by "The Old Professor," manager Casey Stengel, the 1950s Yankees won, and won, and won.

This page: *Yogi Berra hurls himself into Don Larsen's arm seconds after Dodger pinch hitter Dale Mitchell took a called third strike to seal the perfect game.* Opposite page: *Larsen helps Berra hold the glove used to catch the perfect game (no, it was not a Gold Glove). A poor receiver early on in his career, Berra was aided by Bill Dickey to become a fine one.*

A 30-40 lifetime pitcher, for one
day Don Larsen was the best
pitcher to ever step on the rubber
in World Series history.

LEW BURDETTE WINS THREE COMPLETE GAMES IN SERIES

Although the great Warren Spahn spearheaded the 1957 staff of the National League pennant-winning Milwaukee Braves, it was righthander Lew Burdette (17-9 during the season) who pitched the Braves to the World Championship against the New York Yankees.

Milwaukee boasted a powerhouse offense—Hank Aaron (who blasted 44 homers, knocked in 132 runs, and batted .322), third baseman Eddie Mathews, outfielder Wes Covington, and first baseman Joe Adcock. Even though New York could counter with a mighty lineup of its own—Mickey Mantle, Yogi Berra, Moose Skowron, and Gil McDougald—1957 was one of the few times a Yankee World Series opponent appeared more imposing than the Bronx Bombers.

The roar of the Braves' attack was silenced in game one by the great Yankees lefthander Whitey Ford, who outpitched Spahn 3-1. Milwaukee desperately needed Burdette to even the Series; he came through, pitching a seven-hit complete game for a 4-2 victory. The teams traded wins in the next two contests, including a 10-inning complete game by Spahn in the fourth bout.

Prior to the pivotal fifth game, stories speculated about Burdette's using the spitball. Even if Burdette didn't throw the illegal pitch, the thought had been placed in the minds of the Yankees hitters, and that gave the pitcher a psychological edge. Ford was sharp, but Burdette was better, winning an excellent 1-0 pitching duel. He allowed seven base hits, but all were singles. It certainly helped that Mantle had to sit out with a bum leg.

The Yankees tied the Series, winning game six 3-2, to set up the seventh-game showdown. Spahn, scheduled to start, came down with the flu. Manager Fred Haney gambled and went with Burdette on just two days' rest. The big righthander responded with another great pitching performance. While he stifled the Yankees' attack, the Braves scored four runs in the third inning against Don Larsen (last year's Series hero for pitching a perfect game), knocking him out of the game. With the Braves up 5-0 in the bottom of the ninth, the Yankees loaded the bases with two out. Haney stuck with Burdette. Moose Skowron hit a shot down the third-base line that was stabbed by Mathews and turned into a game-ending force play. It was the 24th consecutive scoreless inning for Burdette, who had pitched his second straight shutout.

Although the Yankees outhit the Braves 57-47, Burdette's three complete-game victories made the difference. He gave up only four bases on balls while striking out 13 batters in the 27 innings that he pitched. He allowed 21 base hits and a 0.67 ERA, bringing the Braves franchise its first championship since the 1914 "miracle" team (when they were in Boston) and earning Burdette Series Most Valuable Player honors.

Lew Burdette was the first hurler to throw two shutouts in a World Series since Christy Mathewson in 1905. A product of the Yankee farm system, Burdette was shipped to the Braves along with $50,000 in August 1951 in return for Johnny Sain.

HARVEY HADDIX HURLS PERFECT GAME BUT LOSES

Harvey Haddix

When 35-year-old Pittsburgh Pirates pitcher Harvey Haddix woke up on the morning of May 26, 1959, his head was aching from a bad cold. When Haddix went to sleep that night, it was his heart that was aching. He had just produced one of the greatest pitching performances in baseball history—and lost.

Despite the cold and a cough, Haddix made his scheduled start against the Braves at Milwaukee, and showed no effects of the illness. It was the Braves hitters who looked sick. Haddix used his fastball and slider to turn back the fearsome Hank Aaron, Eddie Matthews, Joe Adcock, and the rest of the Milwaukee lineup inning after inning.

Though Haddix later said that he unaware of it, the crafty lefthander was pitching a perfect game going into the ninth inning. He thought for sure he had walked a couple of hitters. The only problem for Harvey was that the Pirates weren't scoring any runs off Braves starter Lew Burdette. Bill Virdon got to third base for the Bucs in the top of the ninth, but didn't score, so even Haddix knew that a nine-inning perfecto wouldn't be enough to win. He got the first two outs that inning before Burdette, batting for himself, yelled out, "I'll break up your no-hitter." Burdette struck out and Haddix had pitched only the eighth perfect game since 1876. When he retired Johnny O'Brien in the 10th, Haddix became the first pitcher ever to retire 28 batters in a row in one game.

Haddix made even more history thanks to his team's inability to score a run off Burdette. After keeping the Braves hitless through the 10th, 11th, and 12th innings, Haddix became the first pitcher to hurl a no-hitter for more than 11 innings. The Pirates, meanwhile, got their 12th hit off Burdette in the top of the 13th, but didn't score. When Bucs manager Danny Murtaugh suggested Haddix call it a night, the pitcher refused to quit, saying, "I want to win this thing."

In the bottom of the 13th, Braves second baseman Felix Mantilla hit a grounder to third and reached on a throwing error, the first of 37 batters that Haddix pitched to who was able to get on base. Then Matthews sacrificed Mantilla to second and Aaron was walked intentionally. Big Joe Adcock then sent Haddix's second pitch—"my only bad one all game"—over the left field fence for a game-winning homer. Haddix's masterpiece, which would become more famous than most no-hitters, was lost.

In a bizarre ending to the game, Aaron, who thought that the ball had dropped in front of the fence, headed back to the dugout after touching second. Adcock was called out when he reached third base, and the official score of the game was 1-0.

Harvey Haddix is being consoled by Pirates manager Danny Murtaugh (top) as he leaves the field a loser after hurling 12 perfect innings. Bottom: Haddix, the winner of three consecutive Gold Gloves (1958 to 1960), was also regarded as one of the best hitting pitchers of his time.

BILL MAZEROSKI'S BLAST WINS SERIES FOR PIRATES

The 1960 World Series between the New York Yankees and Pittsburgh Pirates was a rematch of the 1927 Series, the last time the Bucs had been to the fall classic. Thirty-three years later, the Pirates must have felt they were facing "Murderer's Row" all over again. With Mickey Mantle and Roger Maris leading the way, the Yankees set Series records for batting (.338) and home runs (10). They also set marks in outhitting the Pirates 91 to 60 and outscoring them 55 to 27. But one swing of Pirates second baseman Bill Mazeroski's bat made all those records footnotes in history.

The Series was tied 3-3 after six games because the Yankees scored most of their runs in their three victories, 16-3, 10-0, and 12-0. The Pirates won their three games by more reasonable scores of 6-4, 3-2, and 5-2.

In game seven at Pittsburgh's Forbes Field, however, Pittsburgh took a page out of the Bombers' book, scoring four runs in the first two innings. Pirates first baseman Rocky Nelson smashed a two-run shot in the first inning. Yankees reliever Bobby Shantz held the Bucs at bay through the middle frames, while his team unlimbered its powerful attack. Home runs by Bill Skowron and Yogi Berra in the fifth and sixth, respectively, made it 5-4 Yankees, and two more runs in the eighth gave New York a three-run edge.

But the Pirates fought back in the bottom of the eighth, helped by some luck. A Bill Virdon grounder, which looked like a sure double play, took a bad hop and hit shortstop Tony Kubek in the throat. Then a Dick Groat single drove in one run. Roberto Clemente beat out an infield hit that scored Virdon. The next man up, catcher Hal Smith, blasted a three-run homer to put Pittsburgh up 9-7.

Buc pitcher Bob Friend couldn't hold the lead in the ninth. Bobby Richardson and Dale Long each singled. Pittsburgh hurler Harvey Haddix came on, but surrendered a single to Mantle, scoring Richardson. Yogi Berra grounded to Nelson, who made a spectacular play and stepped on first. When Nelson fired to second to double Mantle, Gil McDougald (pinch-running for Long) waltzed in from third to tie it at 9-9.

Mazeroski led off the bottom of the ninth for the Pirates. Maz, who was known as a great fielding second baseman, was having a fine offensive Series. His two-run homer in game one proved to be the winning hit. He had smacked six other hits, including two doubles. Now he was facing righthander Ralph Terry; Maz smacked the reliever's second pitch over left fielder Berra's head and into the seats to win the game and the Series. The more than 36,000 fans erupted, and it seemed like half of them went to greet baseball's newest legend at home plate.

Pandemonium reigns in Forbes Field as Bill Mazeroski approaches the plate carrying the run that will give the Pirates their first World Championship since 1925. While not known as a power hitter, Maz slugged 138 career homers even though he played half of his games at sizable Forbes Field.

ROGER MARIS SLUGS 61 HOME RUNS

When Roger Maris began to close in on Babe Ruth's record for the number of home runs in a single season in 1961, he was fighting more than history. In the 34 years since Ruth had hit his 60 homers in 1927, he had come to be regarded as a baseball god. Most fans were horrified at the idea of a mere mortal challenging the Babe's holiest record. By season's end, Commissioner Ford Frick had a pronouncement that an asterisk would be placed next to Maris's record if it took him more than 154 games—the length of a season in Ruth's time—to reach 60.

The years that have passed since 1961 haven't helped Maris's reputation; if anything, it has dropped a notch or two. For one thing, Maris may have been an excellent right fielder, good enough to win two MVP Awards on Yankee teams that featured Whitey Ford, Yogi Berra, and Mickey Mantle—but any comparison of Maris to Ruth is inappropriate. Ruth batted .356 in 1927, 87 points higher than Maris's 1961 average. Maris's career-high in batting was .283; Ruth didn't hit as low as the .280s until his last full season, when he was 40. The colorless Maris also failed to measure up to the Bambino in the area of press relations. While Ruth was outrageous, charming, and an endless source of good newspaper copy, Maris was brusque and testy, or worse. As the march toward the record progressed, his relationship with the press deteriorated.

Maris had another problem: the popular Mantle, who also made a run at Ruth's record in '61. The Yankee fans added to the mounting pressure on Maris by rooting vigorously for Mantle. In mid-July, Maris narrowly led Mantle, who batted behind him in the cleanup position, 35 homers to 33. By September 13, Maris was up 56 to 53. Mantle then fell off the pace because of an injury and ended the season with 54. Maris was still four homers short of tying Ruth by game number 154, which was only a week away. Unable to escape from an oppressive barrage of media and public attention and with his hair falling out from nerves, Maris nevertheless continued to hit home runs. In game 154, he smashed his 59th homer and came within one long foul ball off Orioles pitcher Dick Hall of tying Ruth in the Babe's Baltimore hometown.

Six days later, Maris hit his 60th and, after taking a day off to regroup emotionally, hit number 61 into the right field seats at Yankee Stadium off Boston's Tracy Stallard on the last day of the season. Finally showing joy, Maris danced and celebrated his way around the bases and, for once, the crowd at the Stadium cheered him.

Today, Frick's asterisk has been forgotten. Maris's career may be underrated, but his record no longer is.

A closeup shot of Roger Maris unleashing his all-out swing for his 61st home run to top Babe Ruth. So geared to aiming for the fences in 1961 was Maris that he collected just 151 hits, the fewest of any player who hit over 50 homers in a season, let alone more than 60.

Jim Gentile had a career-best 46 homers due to expansion.

Baseball expansion

The AL expanded in 1961 by adding teams in Washington and Los Angeles. A year later, the NL granted new franchises to New York and Houston. The new ten-team, one-division structure presented competitive problems reminiscent of the old 12-team National League of the 1890s, when one executive lamented: "How can you sell a twelfth-place team?" This quandary was remedied only after a second wave of expansion brought divisional play in 1969.

Expansion also required that the schedule be lengthened to 162 games. Interestingly, the debate over how the new schedule would affect the record books began before Roger Maris neared 60 home runs. In spring of 1961, veteran sportswriter Joe Williams predicted that the additional eight games would soon spell the end for Babe Ruth's home run record.

Roger Maris was not a one-dimensional fence buster. He was a team player who would give himself up to move a runner. And he was a fine fielder who, in 1960, won a Gold Glove Award.

Opposite page, top: *Roger Maris blasts his record-tying 60th homer on September 26 off Jack Fisher of the Orioles.* Opposite page, bottom: *Only Yogi Berra and the batboy greeted Maris when he toed home plate after hitting his 61st.* This page: *Maris's career is often compared to that of Hack Wilson, the NL season homer record holder. But unlike Wilson, Maris was productive for several more seasons.*

MAURY WILLS STEALS
104 BASES

One year after Roger Maris topped Babe Ruth's single-season home run record, another venerable baseball record came crashing down: Ty Cobb's single-season milestone of 96 stolen bases. Set in 1915, Cobb's mark had stood for 57 years, 23 years longer than Ruth's, before Dodger shortstop Maury Wills stole 104 bases in 1962.

Originally a pitcher, Wills was rejected by a Giants scout who said, "There's no such thing as a 155-pound pitcher." Signed by the Dodgers as a shortstop, Wills lacked consistent hitting ability. Major league teams had little use for his speed, because of the static offensive philosophy of the 1950s. Wills spent eight years in the minors before playing his first full season with the Dodgers in 1960 at age 27. Two years later, the baseball world began to notice that Wills, who had stolen 50 bases in only 100 games, was a serious threat to Cobb's record.

On August 26, Wills stole his 72nd; suddenly, much like Maris the previous year, Wills came under tremendous mental and physical strain. He played through foot injuries, hitting slumps, and a bad right hamstring to reach 95 steals in 154 games. Commissioner Ford Frick chose that moment to revive his ridiculous asterisk idea (putting an asterisk next to a record to show that there was a different number of games played), which posterity has fortunately ignored. Wills passed Cobb in game 156—actually the number of games Cobb played in 1915 because of two replayed ties. Wills added numbers 101 to 104 in the three-game pennant playoff against the Giants. Even though the Dodgers lost the pennant, Wills was voted MVP over Willie Mays (who hit 49 homers) and Dodger teammate Tommy Davis (who had 153 RBI).

In a historical sense, Wills's record was a more significant achievement than that of Maris, who was a power-hitter in a power-hitting era. By reviving the art of basestealing, Wills changed the face of the game. The stolen base had lain dormant as an offensive tactic since 1920, when Ruth showed how to score runs in bunches with one swing of the bat. It bottomed out in the NL in 1938, when Stan Hack led with only 18 swipes. Wills led the league in 1960 and 1961 with only 50 and 35 stolen bases, respectively.

Wills led the NL in stolen bases three more times after 1961, and stole 94 in 1965. He retired in 1972 with 586 career stolen bases, then good for fifth on the all-time list, behind dead-ball stars Cobb, Eddie Collins, Max Carey, and Honus Wagner. In the succeeding two decades, however, Wills has been pushed down on the list by his followers: Lou Brock (who broke Wills's season record with 118 steals in 1974), Rickey Henderson (who broke Brock's record with 130 in 1982), Joe Morgan, and Tim Raines. It is clear that Maury Wills's brand of baseball is here to stay.

Maury Wills tied Ty Cobb's single-season stolen base record of 96 with this steal (top) *on September 23 against the St. Louis Cardinals. Cobb set his record in 1915.* Bottom: *Wills wasn't reckless in his pursuit of the record. He was caught stealing only 13 times in his 117 attempts.*

CARDINALS GRAB FLAG AS PHILLIES LOSE 10 STRAIGHT

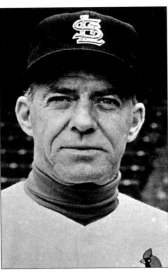

Cardinals manager Johnny Keane

The collapse of the Philadelphia Phillies in 1964 was one of the most memorable fiascoes in baseball. The National League yielded one of the most turbulent pennant races in history. With Philadelphia in front of the pack by six and one-half games and only 12 games left to play, the residents of "the City of Brotherly Love" geared up for the World Series.

Philadelphia's squad was led by Rookie of the Year third baseman Dick Allen (29 homers and 91 RBI), outfielder Johnny Callison (31 homers and 104 RBI), and the keystone combination of second baseman Tony Taylor and shortstop Bobby Wine. The pitching staff had 19-game winner Jim Bunning (who threw a perfect game against the Mets), 17-game winner Chris Short, and 12-game winners Art Mahaffey and Dennis Bennett. The Phillies indeed appeared to be sitting pretty.

Then Philadelphia started losing ugly, as their hitting and pitching fell apart. Beginning on September 18, the Phillies lost 12 of 15 games, including 10 straight. To make matters worse, two games were lost on steals of home and another was given away on a dropped fly ball. Even manager Gene Mauch was not immune to choking. As the slide took hold, Mauch began pitching his aces Bunning and Short on two days' rest. Each lost the three games he pitched on the new schedule.

In the meantime, the Phillies' competition took full advantage of the opportunity. With a lineup that featured Frank Robinson, Vada Pinson, and Deron Johnson, the Cincinnati Reds won nine in a row. The St. Louis Cardinals won eight in succession to make it a three-team race to the wire. The Phils pulled themselves together enough to win their last two games, but the Cards, who had already clinched a tie with Cincinnati two days earlier, beat the New York Mets 11-5 on the final day to seize the flag. Philadelphia beat the Reds on the final day to finish in a tie for second with Cincinnati at 92-70, one game out of first.

The Cardinals added rookie Lou Brock to their roster during the season, and he responded by hitting .348 for St. Louis. Third baseman Ken Boyer led the league with 119 RBI. He also batted .295 with 24 homers and 100 runs scored while winning MVP honors. St. Louis' lineup included first baseman Bill White (.303 average and 102 RBI), center fielder Curt Flood (NL-leading 211 base hits), and shortstop Dick Groat (35 doubles and 70 RBI). The Cardinals rotation included Ray Sadecki (20-11), Bob Gibson (19-12), and Curt Simmons (18-9). The Cardinals beat the Yankees in the World Series four games to three, making St. Louis a champion for the first time since 1946. The Phillies had never won a World Series. To this day, many heartbroken Phillies fanatics still blame Mauch for blowing the pennant.

Ken Boyer was the Cardinals team captain and main catalyst for the St. Louis team winning the pennant in 1964. After Boyer hit a home run in game seven of the '64 fall classic, his brother Clete hit a tater, the first time brothers have had homers in the same World Series game.

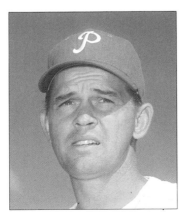

Gene Mauch

Though Gene Mauch had a 1902-2037 lifetime managerial record with four teams over 26 years (Philadelphia, Montreal, Minnesota, and California), he was respected as one of the most astute baseball tacticians. He was named Manager of the Year three times, in 1961, 1964, and 1973. He was famous for playing everyone on his roster and knowing the contents of the baseball rule book, inside and out.

Mauch did take two Angels teams to AL West titles (in 1982 and '86), only to lose the American League Championship Series both times. Mauch, who had also managed the Phillies' choke season of 1964, will be remembered as the best manager never to win a pennant.

HOUSTON'S ASTRODOME OPENS

Astro Jimmy Wynn, Houston's career homer leader (223)

Expansion has brought about divisional playoffs and lengthened the schedule from 154 games to 162. Of all the consequences of expansion, though, none has changed the game of baseball in more ways than the building of the Houston Astrodome.

From the start, owner Judge Roy Hofheinz knew that baseball did not belong outdoors in Houston, Texas. When the nation's first domed stadium could not be completed in time for the first game of the Houston Colt .45s (the original name of the Astros), everyone else knew that baseball didn't belong outdoors in Houston, too. Playing their first three seasons in a temporary park in the middle of a swamp that is now the Astrodome parking lot, the Colts and their fans suffered miserable heat and humidity. The park's nickname "Mosquito Heaven" speaks for itself.

Few fans came to see the new team, but the whole city watched with interest as the nearby dome rose up. On April 9, 1965, Yankee Mickey Mantle christened the park during an exhibition game with the first indoor home run. Three days later, the Houston Astrodome hosted its first official Opening Day game. The Phillies won 2-0 on Dick Allen's homer. Called "The Eighth Wonder of the World," the Astrodome featured an Old-West style bar, luxury skyboxes, and a 474-foot wide scoreboard that produced a 45-second electric light show after every Astro homer. The Astrodome has always retained a flavor that is part amusement park and part science fiction. In 1965, the New York Mets protested that the Astros were using the air-conditioning system to manipulate air currents in a way favorable to the home team. On June 10, 1974, Mike Schmidt launched a massive drive in which a 500-foot homer was transformed into a single when the ball struck a speaker located on the ceiling, 329 feet away from home plate.

The Astrodome originally had a grass developed for indoor use. It flourished under the 4,796 translucent ceiling panels that made up the structure's 208-foot-high roof. It was then discovered that fielders looking up into the ceiling couldn't see fly balls. When the panels were painted over, the grass died. The judge had it replaced with a specially commissioned type of carpet—AstroTurf.

The Astrodome devastates offenses. With its poor visibility and distant fences, the Astros and their opponents have frequently hit fewer than 60 home runs in a season there. In 1981, Houston pitchers and the dome kept opponents to a 2.08 runs per game average—*including* unearned runs—to break the home record of 2.28 set by the Chicago White Sox in 1906. Nevertheless, the Astrodome has begotten other domes, and artificial turf is now found in five open stadiums along with the five domes. Turf has helped alter baseball in ways that are still being understood.

A panoramic view of the Astrodome's interior (top). *Houston fans have seen about everything conceivable happen in it—except a World Series game.* Bottom: *Houston fans were treated to Willie Mays's 500th career home run, hit in the Astrodome on September 13, 1965.*

FRANK ROBINSON FIRST TO WIN MVP IN BOTH LEAGUES

Frank Robinson began his illustrious career with the Cincinnati Reds in 1956 by hitting 38 home runs (tying a rookie record set by Wally Berger in 1930), scoring an NL-leading 122 runs, and taking the Rookie of the Year Award. Even then, even in a league that boasted such players as Willie Mays and Hank Aaron, it seemed inevitable that Robinson would be a future Most Valuable Player.

Over his next four seasons in Cincy, Robby was one of the game's most consistent run producers, averaging 32 home runs, 92 RBI, and 95 runs scored, and batting over .300 in 1957 and '59. He didn't fully explode until 1961, however, when he led the Reds to an NL pennant and won the MVP on the strength of 37 homers, 124 RBI, 117 runs scored, a .323 batting average, and a .611 slugging percentage (he also stole 22 bases).

Robinson sustained that solid pace over the next four seasons, racking up the kind of numbers that today would earn a player millions. His best year, statistically, was in 1962. That season, he belted 39 homers, had 136 RBI (third best in the NL), and posted a .342 average.

The Reds rewarded Robby—the team's best hitter—by trading him to the Baltimore Orioles for pitcher Milt Pappas (and hurler Jack Baldschun and outfielder Dick Simpson) prior to the 1966 season. Depending on what side it is viewed from, it was either one of the best or worst trades in baseball history.

The Orioles were a solid team in the early 1960s, but the acquisition of Robinson, a team leader that they needed, made them unstoppable. A man of great pride, Robby wanted to prove the Reds had made a mistake in dealing him, and prove them wrong he did. He led the American League in home runs (49), RBI (122), and batting average (.316) to take the coveted Triple Crown. He also topped the junior circuit in runs scored (122), on-base percentage (.415), total bases (367), and slugging percentage (.637). He was in the top five in base hits (182), doubles (34), and walks (87). Robinson's tremendous offensive season and his considerable leadership earned him the league's MVP Award, the only player to win that honor in both leagues.

The Orioles, with great pitching, staunch defense, and Robinson's power, won the pennant—their first since moving from St. Louis (they were the Browns) in 1954.

Robinson didn't stop there. In the Orioles' four-game World Series sweep of the Los Angeles Dodgers, he hit two homers. His first, a two-run blast off Don Drysdale in the first inning of game one, set the tone for the Series. His second, again off Drysdale, in game four proved to be the only run of the contest. Robinson was named the World Series MVP.

Frank Robinson was the last righthanded hitter to win a Triple Crown. Three years later, in 1969, he became the first player to lead each major league in being hit by pitches. A good base runner, Robinson scored 1,829 runs to rank 10th on the all-time list and swiped 204 bases.

SANDY KOUFAX WINS FIFTH STRAIGHT ERA TITLE

In 1966, Sandy Koufax won 27 games, lost nine, and won the National League's earned run average title for the fifth straight year with a microscopic 1.73. In 1967, Sandy Koufax was out of baseball.

At what seemed to be the height of his reign, the overpowering lefthander of the Los Angeles Dodgers was forced to retire at age 31 after pitching—and winning big—with an arthritic left elbow for nearly three seasons. His departure concluded one of the most extraordinary pitching careers ever.

Koufax signed with his hometown Brooklyn Dodgers in 1954 at the age of 19. His record over his first seven years in the majors—he never played minor league ball—was just 54-53. He could throw a fastball through a wall, but couldn't hit a spot drawn on that wall. He was the epitome of wildness in a pitcher. After a dismal 8-13 season in 1960, Koufax almost quit the game. Then, Dodgers catcher Norm Sherry spotted a flaw in Koufax's delivery. Like magic, he became a dominant hurler with an explosive fastball and sharply breaking curve.

For the next five years, Koufax was arguably the greatest pitcher baseball has ever seen. His record over that period was 111 wins and 34 loses, for an incredible .761 winning percentage, and a 1.98 ERA. Koufax also led the NL in shutouts three times, averaged 289 strikeouts per year (including an NL-record 382 in 1965), and threw an unprecedented four no-hitters (a record that was broken by Nolan Ryan in 1981). His last no-hitter, in '65, was a perfect game.

"Trying to hit Sandy Koufax in those years," said Pittsburgh slugger Willie Stargell, "was like trying to drink coffee with a fork."

Koufax's first good year came in 1961, when he was 18-13 and led the league in strikeouts. In 1962, he was 14-7 with a 2.54 ERA, his first earned run average crown. His best season, however, was 1963. He went 25-5 to win his first of three Cy Young Awards and his only Most Valuable Player Award. In the Dodgers' 1963 World Series sweep against the New York Yankees, Koufax set a record (since broken) for strikeouts in one game (15). He also set or tied four-game Series marks in starts, complete games, innings (18), and strikeouts (23).

Koufax kept up his awesome pace in 1964, winning 19, losing five, and notching a 1.74 ERA. In 1965, he went 26-8, had a career-high 382 Ks, and a 2.04 earned run average.

Arthritis began afflicting his left shoulder as early as 1962. His last three seasons, Koufax often had to pack his arm in ice for a half hour after a game. After the 1966 season, he retired to save his arm from permanent damage.

No pitcher since has produced a string of seasons to equal his dominant years. For one shining half-decade, Koufax may have been the best pitcher baseball has seen.

Sandy Koufax throwing before his last game, a 6-0 loss to Jim Palmer and the Orioles in game two of the 1966 World Series. A month later, Koufax's arthritic elbow made him decide to call it quits.

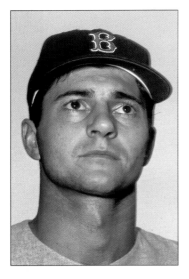

CARL YASTRZEMSKI LEADS RED SOX TO PENNANT

The Boston Red Sox were already looking more like a second-division team during the late 1950s, and the retirement of Ted Williams after the 1960 season only accelerated the process. From 1960—when they were 32 games out of first place—until 1967, the BoSox never won more than 76 games.

Boston finished in ninth place in 1966, 26 games out of first place. The BoSox hope for the future, though, was in the person of young Carl Yastrzemski, who came up in 1961 heralded as "the next Ted Williams." While Yaz wasn't as splendid a splinter as Williams, he was no slouch, either. Yaz led the league in batting his third season and hit over .300 again in 1965. Other than this lefthanded-hitting right fielder, the Red Sox offered their fans little excitement.

Little excitement until 1967, that is. The Red Sox hired the tough Dick Williams as manager before the season got underway. The team—which already had a solid young nucleus with Yaz, third baseman Rico Petrocelli, and outfielder Tony Conigliaro—started rookies Mike Andrews at second base and Reggie Smith in center field and made righthander Jim Lonborg the ace of the pitching staff. Andrews helped anchor the infield, Smith hit 15 homers, and Lonborg won 22 games and the American League Cy Young Award.

But the real story of the '67 Red Sox was Yastrzemski, who produced one of the most glorious seasons ever. Yaz not only led the AL in batting average (.326), home runs (44), and RBI (121) to win the coveted Triple Crown—he also led the league in hits, total bases, on-base percentage, and slugging average to capture Most Valuable Player honors. "For that one season," said Dick Williams, "there could not have been a better baseball player." Shouldered by Yaz and his productive bat, the Red Sox did the near impossible: They went from next-to-last place all the way to first in one season.

Not that the pennant race was easy. It was, in fact, a dogfight to the wire. Boston ultimately took the crown by just one game, thanks primarily to Yaz, who in the last two weeks of a four-team battle (with the Minnesota Twins, Detroit Tigers, and Chicago White Sox) batted .523 with five home runs and 15 RBI. In the final two games of the regular season against the Twins, Yaz banged out hits in seven of his nine at-bats and made countless superb defensive plays in the outfield.

Unfortunately for Boston fans, their team couldn't carry the dream season to a championship. They lost to the St. Louis Cardinals in seven games, but through no fault of Yastrzemski's. Yaz continued his career year in the fall classic, batting .400 with three homers (two in game two) and five RBI.

Carl Yastrzemski batting in game two of the 1967 fall classic (top). He hit two homers that game. Bottom: Yastrzemski would have been the unanimous winner of the 1967 AL MVP Award if one New York writer had not voted, rather quixotically, for Cesar Tovar of the Twins, a .267 hitter.

Bob Gibson wins three games in 1967 Series

Bob Gibson already knew plenty about World Series heroics going into the 1967 fall classic. In the 1964 St. Louis Cardinals' World Series victory over the New York Yankees, Gibby had won two games, including the clincher. He bettered that performance in the 1967 Series against the Boston Red Sox, carrying the Cardinals to a championship on his strong right arm with three victories.

Gibson pitched complete games in games one, four, and—after Boston had just won two games to tie the Series—seven. He struck out 26 batters, total, and yielded just 14 hits and three runs for a Series ERA of 1.00. Nobody was more deserving of the Series MVP than Gibby.

DENNY McLAIN AMASSES 31 WINS

The 1968 season will always be known as "The Year of the Pitcher." It was a year in which one hurler (Bob Gibson) produced a microscopic earned run average of 1.12, another (Don Drysdale) set a record with 58 consecutive scoreless innings, and a third (Denny McLain) won 30 games for the first time in 34 years. It was also a season in which an American League batting title was won with an average just over .300 (.301 by Carl Yastrzemski).

When the confident and colorful Dizzy Dean won 30 games for the St. Louis Cardinals in 1934, four of those were in relief (as were four of the 31 Lefty Grove won three years earlier). When the confident and colorful 24-year-old McLain won 31 in leading the Detroit Tigers to a pennant, all the victories came as a starter.

Ironically, the Tigers tried to trade him when he went 17-16 in 1967, after posting a 20-win season in '66. It was one of those proverbial "the best trades are the ones not made." Although McLain went 0-2 in his first two starts, he had won his 15th game by July 3. Pitching every fourth day, McLain notched his 20th victory on July 27, becoming the first pitcher to win 20 by August 1 since Grove. Overall, the hard-throwing righthander would win 23 of his next 26 decisions.

McLain's unusual success in 1968 was twofold. He added a slider to his sidearm fastball and curve, making him especially tough on righthanded hitters. He also had terrific offensive support. With a lineup of such hitters as Al Kaline, Norm Cash, Willie Horton, and Bill Freehan, the Tigers led the league in runs, totaling 57 more than any other team.

McLain went for win 30 in the September 14 game against Oakland. Although Dizzy Dean was in the stands and the game was nationally televised, McLain didn't seem up to the task. In the top of the ninth inning, Reggie Jackson's second homer of the game had put the A's up 4-3. The Tigers, however, were not surrendering. Kaline, pinch-hitting for McLain, walked and Mickey Stanley singled, putting the winning run on. An infield error tied the game and Horton won it with a blast to left field.

McLain won his next start for number 31, taking, in the process, the Cy Young and MVP awards. He ended the season by leading the AL with 28 complete games, 336 innings pitched, and an .838 winning percentage. He was in the top five in the league with a 1.96 ERA and 280 strikeouts.

McLain followed that sterling season with a 24-9 year and another Cy Young honor. He was suspended once in February of 1970 by Commissioner Bowie Kuhn for being involved in bookmaking and then again in September for possession of a gun. McLain lost 21 games in 1971 and was out of baseball at age 28 in 1972.

Denny McLain wins his 30th game September 14, beating Oakland 5-4. Granted, 1968 was a pitchers' year, but the only other hurler that season who won more than 22 games was Juan Marichal with 26. Success came quickly to McLain and disappeared just as swiftly. His first major league hit was a home run—he never hit another.

Don Drysdale's scoreless innings streak

Although there were several great performances in 1968, the top individual achievement likely was the 58 consecutive scoreless innings streak of the Los Angeles Dodgers' great righthander, Don Drysdale.

Beginning on May 14 and lasting until the third inning on June 8,

"Double D" threw a major league record six shutouts, breaking Carl Hubbell's NL record of 46 straight scoreless innings and Walter Johnson's major league mark of 56. The string was almost broken on May 31 when Drysdale hit Giants catcher Dick Dietz with the bases loaded and none out. It was ruled that Dietz made no attempt to avoid the pitch, and the streak was saved. Drysdale didn't continue his outstanding pitching, finishing the season at 14-12.

Mickey Lolich

TIGERS REBOUND FROM 3-1 TO ECLIPSE CARDS IN WORLD SERIES

The 1968 World Series between the Detroit Tigers and the St. Louis Cardinals was billed as a battle of baseball's two best pitchers, Cy Young Award-winners Denny McLain and Bob Gibson. In the end, however, it was a portly lefthander named Mickey Lolich who stole the spotlight in Detroit's tremendous comeback in the Series.

Game one was all Gibson, as the speedballing righthander shut out the Tigers on five hits and set a World Series record for strikeouts with 17. Detroit bounced back in game two behind the 17-game winner Lolich, who pitched a six-hitter in an 8-1 victory. St. Louis won the next two games in Detroit, 7-3 and 10-1, the latter behind Gibson's second straight complete game (McLain lasted only two and two-thirds innings). It seemed as if a second straight title was in the Cards.

Lolich again came through in the clutch in game five for the beleaguered Tigers, this time with a 5-3 complete game win. The turning point of the Series may have occurred in the fifth inning, when outfielder Willie Horton nailed the speedy Lou Brock at the plate on Brock's failure to slide.

Detroit manager Mayo Smith made an interesting and critical decision for game six. He brought back his ace McLain, who had barely broken loose in game four before he was knocked out, on two days' rest—and the 31-game winner finally delivered. McLain's nine-hit complete game in a 13-1 win gave the team much-needed momentum. The Tigers scored 10 runs in the third; the highlight of the inning was Jim Northrup's grand slam.

Game seven pitted Gibson against Lolich, and the two hurlers engaged in a superb scoreless pitching duel for the first six innings. Gibson struck out Lolich in the third, racking up his 32nd strikeout of the Series and, in the process, breaking his own record set in 1964—he ended with 35 Ks. In the sixth, the Cardinals threatened, but Brock (who tied a Series record with 13 hits and batted .464) and Curt Flood were both picked off first by Lolich's deceptive lefthanded move.

Those baserunning blunders would come to haunt the Cardinals in the next inning. With two outs in the seventh, Norm Cash and Willie Horton singled off Gibson. Then Northrup tripled and Bill Freehan doubled to put Detroit up 3-0 and stun the 55,000-strong home crowd. While Detroit added a single run in the ninth, only Mike Shannon's two-out homer touched Lolich. Lolich's three victories earned him the Series MVP. Al Kaline and Northrup each smacked two homers and drove in eight runs. Norm Cash added five RBI. Detroit's first title since 1945 made the Tigers the third team in history to overcome a 3-1 deficit and win the World Series.

Mickey Lolich about to deliver during game seven, during which he outdueled Bob Gibson to complete the Tigers comeback from a three-games-to-one deficit. Several players have homered in their first World Series appearance; Lolich is the only one whose Series dinger was the lone four-bagger of his career.

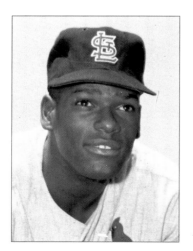

Bob Gibson dominates the National League

Although Denny McLain's 31-victory season in 1968 was certainly an outstanding achievement, it wasn't the year's most dominating pitching performance. The accomplishment was a close second to Bob Gibson's phenomenal 1.12 earned run average, the lowest for a pitcher with more than 300 innings in history and the lowest since Dutch Leonard's 0.96 set in 1914.

In leading the St. Louis Cardinals to the World Series, Gibson won 22 games, completing 28 of the 34 games he started. He won the NL Cy Young Award hands-down, adding a league-leading 268 strikeouts and 13 shutouts. He was in the top five in wins, complete games, and innings (305). Gibson set a World Series record for strikeouts in a game (17) and in a Series (35).

MIRACLE METS ASCEND TO CHAMPIONSHIP

Jerry Koosman

In 1969, New York was being tagged the "Miracle Mets" even before the start of the World Series against the Orioles. Perennial losers, the best season in the Mets' seven-year history had been in 1968 when they were 73-89 and finished ninth. In '69, the Mets parlayed great pitching—led by young Tom Seaver and Jerry Koosman—tight defense, timely hitting, and luck into 100 wins and one of the biggest transformations in baseball.

Beating the Braves three straight in the NLCS was one thing, beating Baltimore was another. It appeared the Orioles would make short work of the Series when they beat Mets ace and 25-game winner Tom Seaver 4-1 in game one.

The Mets, however, spent all season finding ways to win. In game two, Koosman no-hit the Orioles for six innings while trying to make a Donn Clendenon solo homer stand up. The O's scored a run in the bottom of the seventh, but the Mets grabbed the game in the ninth on an RBI single by utility infielder Al Weis.

In game three, rookie righthander Gary Gentry and young Nolan Ryan hurled a shutout at the Birds, thanks to a couple of spectacular catches by center fielder Tommie Agee. With the Mets up 3-0 in the fourth, the Orioles put two on with two out. Elrod Hendricks then belted a Gentry pitch up the left-center field gap and Agee, going full speed toward the wall, nixed the apparent extra-base hit when he backhanded the ball in the webbing of his glove. Then the Orioles loaded the bases in the seventh. Paul Blair hit Ryan's first fastball deep to right center. Agee made a diving catch on the warning track. The two great defensive plays prevented five Orioles runs.

Game four was a pitching duel between Seaver and Baltimore lefty Mike Cuellar. The Mets were leading 1-0 in the top of the ninth when right fielder Ron Swoboda made his own incredible catch. With men on first and third and one out, Brooks Robinson hit a drive to short right center. Swoboda dove and stretched his arm across his body. The ball landed in his glove before he hit the turf. In the bottom of the 10th, the Mets' winning run scored after pinch-hitter J.C. Martin laid down a sacrifice bunt and was hit by the ball as he ran to first.

The inevitable came the next day. The Mets wiped out a 3-0 Orioles lead on a Clendenon two-run homer in the sixth (his third of the Series, which earned him the MVP) and an unlikely second Series homer by Al Weis in the seventh. In the eighth, two doubles and an Orioles error made the Mets champions.

Tom Seaver delivers in the fourth game of the 1969 fall classic. In that game he was masterful, pitching one-run, six-hit ball for a 2-1 Mets victory. The Mets hit only .220 in the Series, but New York pitching kept the Orioles to a measly .146 batting average.

Al Weis

Mets capture improbable wins on road to pennant

In winning their unlikely World Championship, the 1969 Mets were pretty good and very lucky.

One day, they won a double-header against the Pittsburgh Pirates by identical scores of 1-0; and in both games, the Mets' pitchers—Jerry Koosman and Don Cardwell—drove in the winning run. Al Weis hit two homers all season, and each won a game against the second-place Cubs—at Wrigley Field. During their mid-September march to the pennant, they faced Steve Carlton of the St. Louis Cardinals and struck out 19 times for a new record. Then Mets outfielder Ron Swoboda hit two two-run homers to give the Mets a 4-3 victory; he struck out the other two times he batted.

BROOKS ROBINSON'S HOT GLOVE CAPTURES FALL CLASSIC

In the long history of the World Series, nobody had ever turned it into a defensive showcase the way Brooks Robinson did in 1970. The Baltimore Orioles Gold Glove third baseman already had a reputation for being one of the greatest ever at his position. In the five games against the Cincinnati Reds, he proved his supremacy to the world.

The Orioles, who desperately wanted to avenge their previous year's loss to the New York Mets, won game one at Cincy 4-3, but the outcome would have been different if not for the "Human Vacuum Cleaner." With no outs and the score tied in the bottom of the sixth inning, Reds first baseman Lee May hit a smash down the third base line. Robinson, who was a slow runner but incredibly quick at third, backhanded the ball as it appeared to go past him into foul territory. In one motion, he turned and threw off-balance to first, nailing May by a step. In the seventh, Robinson hit what turned out to be the game-winning homer.

Robinson continued his human highlight film act in game two. He dove toward shortstop to turn one potential hit into a force play and backhanded another May grounder that he converted into a double play. Although the Reds scored four runs in those innings, Robinson's plays kept the game close enough for the Orioles to launch a comeback and a 6-5 victory.

His fielding clinic continued in game three, as he continued to show baseball fans how a third baseman makes every possible play. In the first inning, he made a leaping grab of a Tony Perez shot and turned it into two outs. In the second frame, he backhanded Tommy Helms's swinging roller and threw him out by a step. Robinson also continued his great hitting in the Series, going 2-for-4 with two RBI in a 9-3 victory.

The Robinson hitting show was in the spotlight again in game four as Brooks smacked four hits (tying a Series record), including a homer. The Reds, however, went on to take the game 6-5. In game five, Cincinnati jumped to a 3-0 first-inning lead, but the Orioles responded with two runs in each of their first three frames. They were leading 9-3 in the ninth when Robinson provided one last glimpse of his magic at the hot corner—something for the fans to remember him by. He made a diving catch of a Johnny Bench line drive. He also batted .429 with nine hits in five games (tying a record). After the Series, Bench marveled, "I never saw Pie Traynor play, but if he was better at playing third than Brooks Robinson, he had to be inhuman."

Brooks Robinson was dubbed "Hoover" in the 1970 fall classic for making outstanding defensive play after unbelievable defensive play. He was named Series MVP for his all-around play. Robinson tied a World Series record with nine hits in a five-game affair. He had two homers, including a game-winning tater in game one.

Johnny Bench

Big Red Machine

Although the Cincinnati Reds lost the 1970 World Series, their appearance in that fall classic was the beginning of a glorious decade in the oldest franchise's history.

Throughout the 1970s, the Reds possessed baseball's most talented lineup: run-producing first baseman Lee May and then Tony Perez; Hall of Fame second baseman Joe Morgan; All-Star shortstop Dave Concepcion; baseball's all-time hit leader Pete Rose at third and the outfield; slugging left fielder George Foster; excellent right fielder Ken Griffey; and Hall of Fame catcher Johnny Bench. That decade, the Reds took two world titles (1975 and 1976), two pennants (1970 and '72), two West Division crowns, and three second-place finishes.

ROBERTO CLEMENTE IS ASTONISHING IN SERIES

On the field, there was no purer competitor than Pittsburgh Pirate Roberto Clemente. He was a great right fielder with perhaps the best arm among history's outfielders. He regularly collected 20 assists a season and won 12 Gold Gloves. With his exquisite quickness and timing at the plate—and a slashing, inside-out swing that produced line drives—he was a perennial contender for the batting title. It was only off the field, with management, the fans, and the media, that Clemente sometimes seemed out of sync.

From 1961 to 1967, Clemente won four batting titles and drove in or scored 100 runs five times. He won an MVP Award in 1966. But with Pittsburgh never managing to win a pennant, Clemente's status as a star somehow remained shaky.

In 1971, the Pirates won the NL East and defeated San Francisco 3-1 in the NLCS. Clemente hit .341 for the season but played only 132 games as the effects of age, a chronic bad back, and years of playing baseball year-round began to catch up with him. It took the 1971 World Series against Baltimore for Clemente to finally gain the respect he deserved.

Playing with his usual furious hustle, Clemente made impossible diving catches, froze baserunners with his rifle of an arm, and hit .414. Covering the 1971 Series, Roger Angell wrote: "Clemente was playing to win, but also playing the game almost as if it were a form of punishment for everyone else on the field."

With their offense and staff of four 20-game winners, the Orioles were strong favorites; after four games, however, the Series was tied two-all. Continuing a streak he had started in the first game of the 1960 World Series, Clemente had at least one hit in each game. In game five, Nellie Briles two-hit the Orioles and put the Pirates up in the Series, three games to two; again, Clemente had a hit. He came close to eliminating the Orioles in game six. His first-inning triple narrowly missed clearing the left-center field wall and his third inning home run put the Pirates up 2-0. But Baltimore came back to win 3-2. In the fourth inning of the seventh game, Clemente struck again, launching a solo homer. Steve Blass limited the Orioles to four hits and won 2-1. Clemente's 12 hits and five extra-base hits led all hitters; he didn't record a single assist as no Oriole dared try to take an extra base on him. He was the overwhelming choice as Series MVP.

Clemente played only one more season. Killed in a plane crash on his way to bring relief to earthquake-stricken Nicaragua on the last day of 1972, he had a .317 career average on exactly 3,000 hits. The Hall of Fame waived its five-year waiting period and inducted Clemente in 1973.

Roberto Clemente at bat in the 1971 World Series. He had two doubles, a triple, two homers, two bases on balls, three runs scored, four RBI, a .414 batting average, and a .759 slugging percentage in the seven games. A 12-time Gold Glove winner in the outfield, he could have been the greatest fielding flycatcher of all time.

Pirates manager Danny Murtaugh

World Series is first played at night

Night baseball had been technically feasible for almost a half-century before the major leagues reluctantly tried it in the 1930s. By the 1940s and 1950s, regular-season night games were common and extremely popular with the millions of fans who worked five days a week; baseball attendance boomed. Still, tradition dictated that the World Series be played during the day.

Television changed that mindset. By 1960, television had invaded 85 percent of all American households; by 1970, it was paying an ever-increasing share of baseball's freight. Under pressure to move baseball's most important games to prime time, Commissioner Bowie Kuhn chose to schedule game four of the 1971 Series at night as an experiment. An astounding 61 million viewers tuned in to see Pittsburgh even the Series 2-2. From 1972 on, Kuhn ordered, all weekday World Series games were to be played at night.

STEVE CARLTON WINS 27 FOR LAST-PLACE PHILLIES

For four years the St. Louis Cardinals had waited for Steve Carlton to develop into the dominant lefthanded pitcher they thought he'd be when he came up in 1967. He'd constantly tease the Cardinals management with games like that 19-strikeout classic he threw against the New York Mets in 1969. But the Cards also knew they had to be patient, considering the baseball axiom that says lefthanders take longer in developing than righthanders. Finally, in 1971, after a disappointing 10-19 season, Carlton blossomed and went 20-9.

But when Carlton hassled with Cardinal owner Gussie Busch over his contract, the beer baron traded Carlton to the Philadelphia Phillies for their ace righthander Rick Wise. Nobody had to wait three to five years to see who would get the better of this deal. In one year it was called one of the worst trades ever made.

The 1972 Phillies were a terrible team. They won just 59 games and lost 97; only the four-year-old expansion San Diego Padres were as bad. Just imagine how really bad the Phillies would have been without Carlton and his 27 victories. On the days he pitched, Philadelphia played almost like pennant contenders. His victories represented 46 percent of the total wins that Philly earned that year. With him, they played .378 baseball; subtract Carlton's decisions, the Phillies were a .270 team.

"It was really hard to explain," recalled shortstop Larry Bowa, who played behind Carlton that year, once recalled, "but when 'Lefty' was on the mound, we always felt confident we would win. We felt like a different team because he always kept us in the game. I guess we were trying to live up to his excellence."

In winning his first of a record four Cy Young Awards, in 1972, Carlton also won pitching's triple crown, adding NL leads in ERA (1.97) and strikeouts (310) to his league-leading 27 victories, becoming just the 23rd pitcher since 1900 to accomplish the feat. It was one of the greatest pitching seasons in baseball history. He also added league leads in innings pitched (346) and complete games (30)—and he threw eight shutouts and had a .730 winning percentage, second in the league in those categories. He also had a 15-game winning streak. In 1972, and for most of his career, Carlton possessed an excellent fastball and curve. But his out pitch was a devastating slider that was especially tough on righthanded hitters.

The media couldn't get much from Carlton to explain his phenomenal success in '72. Notoriously inaccessible to the press, Carlton eventually stopped talking to reporters altogether by 1978 and was nicknamed "Silent Steve." But he did plenty of talking on the mound. He continued being unhittable for the next 16 years, accumulating 329 lifetime victories and 4,136 strikeouts.

Steve Carlton's 27 wins topped not only the Phillies but also the majors. Here he is putting the finishing touches on win number 27, an 11-1 triumph over the Cubs on the closing day of the season. "Lefty" established a modern record for the most wins by a pitcher on a cellar dweller and fell only two short of the all-time record of 29, set by Matches Kilroy in 1886.

METS CLIMB FROM LAST PLACE TO PENNANT

Yogi Berra

It had been just four years since their "miracle" season, but the Mets were just plain lousy in the first half of the 1973 season. They couldn't score runs for ace Tom Seaver. They weren't getting much production from their offense, which included an aging Willie Mays. Everyone was getting hurt, such as catcher Jerry Grote and shortstop Bud Harrelson, who went on the disabled list twice. Their ace reliever, Tug McGraw, wasn't getting hitters out or saving games. Even manager Yogi Berra was having a tough time coming up with his classic Yogi-isms.

With the team's record at 34-46 in early July, team chairman M. Donald Grant called a meeting and told the club to relax, that it had to believe in itself. The fun-loving McGraw picked up on the speech and began shouting, "Ya Gotta Believe" in the clubhouse. It became the rallying cry for the Mets and their fans.

On August 5, the Mets were 48-60, but the entire NL East was playing mediocre ball, so New York trailed by only 11½ games. On August 29, the Mets escaped the cellar for the first time since late June to pull within five and one-half games. By mid-September, with all their key players healthy, the Mets had cut the deficit to two and one-half going into a crucial set of five games with the division-leading Pirates.

After splitting two in Pittsburgh, the teams were tied 3-3 in the 13th inning of the next game, in New York. Pirate Dave Augustine's potential game-winning home run hit the top of the left field fence, bounced into the glove of Mets outfielder Cleon Jones, who relayed the ball to the infield to nail Richie Zisk at the plate. The Mets won the game in the bottom of the inning. During the next evening's win at Shea Stadium, a fan carried a banner reading: "Give the left field fence a World Series share."

The Mets carried the momentum into first place on September 22. They were leading by a one-half game margin before a three-game season-ending series against the Cubs. On September 30, the Mets clinched a tie for the pennant. They then won the first game of a doubleheader, and the race was over. They had won 34 of their last 53 during the drive, thanks primarily to McGraw, who in 19 games down the stretch saved 12, won five, and had a 0.88 ERA.

The Mets mystery continued into the NLCS, when they beat the heavily favored Cincinnati Reds in five games (which included a famous fight between Harrelson and Pete Rose). But New York fell short in the World Series, losing in seven games to the Oakland A's after taking a 3-2 lead.

Willie Mays demonstrates his opinion of a strike call by umpire Augie Donatelli in the 1973 World Series (top). *The seven-game affair was the 42-year-old Mays's major league coda.* Bottom: *Pete Rose of the Reds pins Mets shortstop Bud Harrelson to the turf after the pair exchanged blows following Rose's hard slide into second base in game three of the NLCS.*

HANK AARON SLAMS HIS 715TH CAREER HOME RUN

During a career that spanned from 1954 through 1976, Hank Aaron was never known as just a home run hitter. He could hit homers, to be sure, leading the NL in four different seasons and belting 44 homers in four seasons. Aaron never hit more than 47 in any season, but the silent superstar was methodical and consistent. "Hammerin' Hank" had a quick, efficient swing, which derived its power from his strong, sinewy wrists.

Aaron walked away with the MVP crown in 1957 (during which he hit a late September home run to give Milwaukee the pennant), batting titles in 1956 and 1959, and a lifetime .364 average in 14 World Series games. It was not until June 10, 1972, however—when Aaron hit his 649th homer to pass Willie Mays and take second place on the all-time list—that his power exploits drew national attention.

Suddenly, there was great interest in the 38-year-old Aaron and in the possibility of his hitting another 66 homers—the number needed to break the lifetime record of 714 round-trippers set by Babe Ruth. "Even if I'm lucky enough to hit 715 home runs," Aaron said modestly, "Babe Ruth will still be regarded as the greatest home run hitter who ever lived."

Going into the 1973 season needing only 42 homers to pass Ruth, Aaron was bombarded by pressure from all sides. "It should have been an enjoyable time," he once recalled, "but instead, everywhere I went people were talking about home runs. And I had no privacy."

Aaron hit No. 713 on the next to the last day of the 1973 season. When the Braves' 1974 season began on the road, the team's owners tried to sit Aaron out. They wanted him to break the record at home. Commissioner Bowie Kuhn ruled that the club would have to play him during its first three games. On April 4, Aaron tied Ruth—on his first swing of the season off Cincinnati Reds pitcher Jack Billingham into left-center field. It had taken Aaron 2,890 more at-bats than the Babe to hit 714 homers.

Four days later, the Braves played a nationally televised game against the Los Angeles Dodgers. There were 53,000 people in the stands at Atlanta Stadium and another 35 million viewers, all hoping to witness history. And Hammerin' Hank didn't let them down. Al Downing walked Aaron on five pitches in the second inning. Then, on his first official at-bat of the game in the fourth inning, he knocked a fastball over the fence in left field for the monumental homer. Aaron had conquered what he called "the Cadillac of baseball records."

Aaron traveled around the bases a few more times before he was through, accumulating 755 homers upon his retirement two years later (as a member of the Milwaukee Brewers).

Hank Aaron unloads on Al Downing's pitch to belt his 715th career home run to break Babe Ruth's record. Eddie Mathews, the Braves manager at the time, was the only member of the home-team audience who had been with the franchise when Aaron hit his first four-bagger back in 1954.

**The media crush on Hank Aaron
was unrelenting. After he hit
the 715th, he said: "Thank God
it's over."**

Opposite page: *Aaron is greeted after his record-tying 714th off Jack Billingham of the Reds on Opening Day in 1974. Billingham was the Reds' top winner that year; Ruth's 714th also came off one of the NL's premier pitchers at the time, Guy Bush. This page: Hank Aaron pulls the trigger on his 715th home run. He hit just 18 more in 1974, and his total of 20 was his lowest since his rookie season.*

MIKE MARSHALL PITCHES IN 106 GAMES

The Los Angeles Dodgers had led the NL West by as many as 11 games in July of 1973, only to be overtaken by Cincinnati. With the primary factor in the slide being a weak bullpen, the Dodgers pushed to strengthen their pitching attack for '74; they traded with the Expos, exchanging outfielder Willie Davis for the righthanded screwballing relief pitcher Mike Marshall.

Marshall had a bit of a screwball personality. A doctor of physiology, he engaged in his own training regimen and intimidated coaches and managers who wouldn't let him maintain his independence. After struggling early in his career, he developed as a reliever under manager Gene Mauch at Montreal.

After three seasons with the Expos, Marshall had won 33 games, saved 70 (leading the league in 1973), and appeared in 223, setting a record for games with 92 in '73. The closest thing to an every-day player a pitcher could be, Marshall was establishing, once and for all, the importance of the short reliever in modern day baseball.

The Dodgers started fast in 1974, racking up a 36-14 record by the end of May. Then from the middle of June until early July, Marshall pitched in a record 13 straight games, winning six in relief. "A lot of guys can probably go out there 13 days in a row," said Jim Brewer, Marshall's bullpen mate, "but I can't think of anyone who could be as effective as Mike was."

The Reds tightened the gap in the pennant race in the West, closing to within one and one-half games as late as September 14. Marshall kept the Dodgers from collapsing as they had the year before. His excellent relief work stopped a six-game losing streak in mid-August and his victories in two games in the last week held off the Reds. "A lot of guys were key to us winning that year," said Dodgers starter Don Sutton, "but Mike was unbelievable."

Marshall ended up breaking his own record for appearances with an astounding 106, relief innings with 208, and games finished with 83. Overall, he saved 21 games, won 15, and was voted both Fireman of the Year and the league's Cy Young Award-winner (the first ever won by a reliever).

The Dodgers defeated the Pirates for the 1974 NL pennant, with Marshall appearing in two games and giving up no runs. Los Angeles lost to the powerful Oakland Athletics in five games in the World Series. Marshall saved the Dodgers' sole victory, only to yield the winning run in the seventh inning of game five after Los Angeles had tied it the previous frame. He pitched in all five games, giving up only one run and striking out 10 in nine innings.

Marshall's 1974 will go down as one of the greatest seasons ever by a relief pitcher.

Mike Marshall pitching in game one of the '74 Series. Even more extraordinary perhaps than his 106 mound appearances in 1974 were the 208 innings he worked in relief; no other reliever besides Marshall has ever toiled more than 168 frames in a season. He also pitched in a modern record 13 straight games in a season.

CARLTON FISK'S HOMER KEEPS BOSTON ALIVE

Simply say the words "game six" and many baseball fans will know what you're talking about. The sixth game of the 1975 World Series between the Cincinnati Reds and the Boston Red Sox is considered the most exciting World Series game ever played—and the Series is regarded as one of the best.

The Reds were leading the Series three games to two going into Boston's Fenway Park on October 21, a contest that had been postponed by rain for three days. The Red Sox jumped in front in the first inning on a three-run homer by American League MVP and Rookie of the Year Fred Lynn. Cagey Cuban righthander Luis Tiant made it hold up until the top of the fifth when the Reds rallied to tie it. The Big Red Machine then engineered two runs in the seventh and one in the eighth to take a 6-3 lead and pin the BoSox to the ropes.

The Beantowners bounced back in the bottom of the eighth. After the first two batters reached base, Reds manager Sparky Anderson summoned reliever Rawly Eastwick, the sixth Cincy pitcher of the game (they would tie a Series record with eight). Eastwick retired the first two batters and had a 3-2 count on lefthanded pinch hitter Bernie Carbo. The former Red fouled off one pitch, then blasted a fastball over the center field fence to tie the game.

In the bottom of the ninth, the Sox loaded the bases with none out. Will McEnaney got Lynn to hit a shallow fly ball to left field. George Foster made the catch and nailed Denny Doyle at the plate trying to score. The game went into extra innings.

The Red Sox turned on their own defensive power in the 11th inning. With one out and one on, Joe Morgan belted the ball to deep right field and Dwight Evans snared it with a leaping one-handed catch. Evans then threw to first baseman Carl Yastrzemski, doubling off Ken Griffey to end the threat.

It was past midnight and reliever Pat Darcy was working his third inning when Red Sox catcher Carlton Fisk led off the 12th. He swung at Darcy's first delivery and hit a high fly ball down the left field line. As the ball traveled on its arc, the television cameras showed Fisk dancing down the line and waving his arms, practically willing the ball to stay fair. The ball hit the foul pole to give Boston an incredible 7-6 victory.

In the seventh game, the Red Sox blew a 3-0 lead and lost to the Reds 4-3 on a run in the ninth inning. Boston had won the game six battle, but Cincinnati had won the war.

Carlton Fisk watches his shot after hitting it. It had the distance; the only question was the placement. "Pudge" and the Red Sox's co-hero in game six, Bernie Carbo, both hit two homers in the Series. In 1972, Fisk tied with Joe Rudi for the AL lead in triples with nine. It was the only time Pudge led the league in an offensive category.

Fred Lynn wins the MVP and Rookie of the Year awards

Although the Boston Red Sox 1975 American League pennant-winning team featured some great veterans, it was carried to the title by the one-two punch of rookies Jim Rice and Fred Lynn. Rice, a righthanded-hitting outfielder, belted 22 homers and knocked in 102 runs. Lynn was even better. The 23-year-old lefthanded-hitting center fielder produced one of the best rookie seasons ever, batting .331 with 21 homers and 105 RBI. Lynn led the league in runs (103) and slugging average (.566). He won the Rookie of the Year and the Most Valuable Player awards, the only player to win both honors in the same year.

This page: *Carlton Fisk lifts Pat Darcy's sinker toward the left field pole. Fisk roars in jubilation* (opposite page, top) *when he sees his 12th-inning four-bagger clear the Green Monster. Red Sox players cluster around home plate to laud Fisk after he extended the Series to a seventh contest* (opposite page, bottom).

Carlton Fisk's shot
was the perfect end
to the perfect game.
It was so good that
the Reds' 4-3 win in
the finale paled by
comparison.

CHRIS CHAMBLISS'S BLAST WINS PENNANT

Parity may be good for football; in baseball, however, the natural order of things seemed to include a New York Yankees dynasty. Starting with Babe Ruth and continuing through the days of Casey Stengel and Mickey Mantle, baseball fans always had great Yankees teams to love or to hate.

Then, in 1965, the Yankees fell to sixth, and in 1966, New York finished dead last, marking the beginning of a decade-long pennant drought.

In December of 1975, arbitrator Peter Seitz released Dave McNally and Andy Messersmith from their contracts, a decision that brought about a new era of free agency. And in 1976, the Yankees returned to postseason play. In many minds, these two events are related. In fact—Catfish Hunter notwithstanding—this new Yankees dynasty was built on trades, not on free-agent signings. In addition to home-grown products outfielder Roy White and catcher Thurman Munson, the 1976 club featured first baseman Chris Chambliss and third baseman Graig Nettles (traded from Cleveland), outfielder Mickey Rivers and hurler Ed Figueroa (from California), second baseman Willie Randolph and pitcher Dock Ellis (from Pittsburgh), outfielder Lou Piniella (from Kansas City), and reliever Sparky Lyle (from Boston).

Back in Yankee Stadium after a two-year exile to Shea and under the management of Stengel-protege Billy Martin, this team stormed past defending division-winner Boston and a fading Orioles dynasty to take the AL East by 10½ games. Facing George Brett, Hal McRae, and the Royals in a five-game ALCS, the two teams alternated victories through game four.

It was Dennis Leonard versus Figueroa in a fifth-game thriller that established the pattern for three straight years' worth of epic New York-Kansas City postseason wars. John Mayberry's homer gave the Royals a 2-0 lead in the first frame. The Yankees tied the score in the bottom of the inning with a Rivers triple and a White single. Chambliss (who had hit .293 with 17 home runs and 96 RBI on the season) then sacrificed White home. The Yankees scored two each in the third and sixth to build a 6-3 lead after seven.

In the top of the eighth, Brett tied the score with a three-run shot off of Grant Jackson. Then, in the bottom of the ninth, Chambliss faced journeyman righthander Mark Littell and drove the first pitch of the inning into the right-center field seats, over the outstretched arm of McRae. Yankee Stadium erupted, and Chambliss had to fight the crowd to circle the bases.

Later, after the crowd had left the field, Chambliss came back on the field and touched home plate, secretly ensuring the home run.

In the World Series, the Yankees didn't fare so well. New York was humiliated in a four-game sweep by the Big Red Machine.

Chris Chambliss crushed the pitch of Mark Littell to give New York the AL pennant. According to Thurman Munson, a celebratory Yankees' crowd prevented Chambliss from tagging home plate after his homer; he had to sneak out of the clubhouse later to touch it and make his pennant-winning run official.

REGGIE JACKSON'S BACK-TO-BACK-TO-BACK TATERS

There were two Reggie Jacksons. One is the Reggie who hit 563 home runs and led the league in homers four times; he also struck out 2,597 times—the most in history—and batted .262 lifetime. The other Reggie was "Reggie the Show," and that one had to be seen to be appreciated.

In October, the two Reggies became one. Jackson played in 11 League Championship Series (batting .227) and five World Series (72 games in all), and his postseason record shows why he was called "Mr. October." He hit 10 career World Series homers—fifth-best of all time—and batted .357, ninth-best. At .755, he is the greatest slugger in World Series history. Jackson homered and drove in six runs for Oakland to become the MVP of the 1973 Series—nothing compared with his 1977 performance, in which he swatted five home runs in six games.

Coming to New York in 1977, Jackson signed one of the first big free-agent deals ($2.96 million over five years). "I didn't come to New York to be a star," he announced. "I brought my star with me." Self-described as "the straw that stirs the drink," his ego ruffled the feathers of such veterans as Thurman Munson and Graig Nettles, who had led the Yankees to the 1976 flag. As it turned out, it was Jackson's 32 home runs and 110 RBI that proved to be critical in a tight 1977 pennant race.

In the World Series, Jackson started slowly, going 1-for-6, as the Yankees and Dodgers split the first two games. He contributed an RBI single in the victory of Mike Torrez over Dodger Tommy John in game three. Jackson was just getting started. In the second inning of game four, his double started a three-run rally and his sixth-inning, opposite-field home run capped a 4-2 New York win. The Dodgers took the next game 10-4, but in the eighth inning Jackson homered again.

The thunder and lightning came early in game six. Facing Burt Hooton his first time up, Jackson walked on four pitches. With a 3-2 lead in the fourth, Hooton made the mistake of throwing a first-pitch strike and Reggie hit it out of the park. The next inning, Reggie homered off reliever Elias Sosa's first pitch to put the Yankees up 7-3. Not even Charlie Hough's knuckleball could stop Reggie in the eighth as he homered again on the first pitch; the Yankees won the game 8-4 and the Series 4-2. Jackson matched Babe Ruth's record of three homers in a World Series game (in both the 1926 and 1928 Series), but not even Ruth had accomplished the feat with only three swings. Counting the last at-bat of game five, Jackson had hit home runs in four consecutive at-bats on only four swings.

Reggie Jackson playing the part of Mr. October. Jackson's .357 career average in fall classic play is almost 100 points more than his lifetime batting average. In the 1977 ALCS, also played in October, he hit just .125 with two singles in 16 at-bats, but all that was forgotten by the time the World Series had ended.

Billy Martin

Reggie Jackson and Billy Martin feud

The Yankees of the "Bronx Zoo" years were long on egos, none bigger than those of Reggie Jackson and Billy Martin. Both came to New York in 1977 with long histories of conflict, and it was only a matter of time before they squared off.

The first confrontation between the slugger and the manager came in June 1977, when Martin replaced Jackson in the middle of an inning after he had botched a fly ball. A national TV audience watched as an enraged Jackson had to be pulled off Martin by Yogi Berra; Jackson was suspended. In July 1978, pouting over being platooned, Jackson refused an order to bunt; then, with the count 0-2 and the bunt-sign off, he bunted foul and struck out. Jackson was suspended again while Martin trumpeted his famous "born liar" remark and was rewarded with the first of his five Yankee firings.

This page: *In 1977, pitching for his fourth team in four seasons, Mike Torrez became the only pitcher between 1976 and 1983 to notch two complete-game wins in a World Series. Reggie Jackson (opposite page) seems almost himself in awe of what he's just done— hit his record-breaking third homer on three swings in the final game of the 1977 Series.*

Reggie Jackson was Series MVP for Oakland in 1973, but it was in 1977 that he became "Mr. October."

BUCKY DENT'S PLAYOFF HOME RUN WINS EAST FOR YANKEES

For the first half of the 1978 AL East pennant race, the Boston Red Sox led comfortably while the defending champion New York Yankees were in disarray. On July 17, New York bottomed out in fourth place, 14 games behind Boston. It would have been worse if not for Ron Guidry, who was winning nearly every start on his way to a 25-3 record. Catfish Hunter's sore arm wouldn't heal, Goose Gossage was ineffective, and Thurman Munson's bad knees prevented him from catching every day. Overshadowing all of this was Billy Martin's running feud with Reggie Jackson, which culminated in Martin's firing on July 24.

Under new manager Bob Lemon's calming presence, the Yankees' luck began to change. Hunter rebounded and started to win, and the bats came alive; the Yankees won 10 of 12 and, later, 16 of 18. In September, the Red Sox lead was down to four games before a four-game home series against New York. With Fred Lynn and Carl Yastrzemski hurt, Boston suffered a second massacre, losing each of the four games in a rout. Boston, however, refused to die. After slipping to three and one-half games behind in mid-September, the BoSox battled back to regain a tie on the last day of the season, forcing a one-game pennant playoff at Fenway.

Guidry took the mound to face 16-game winner Mike Torrez. In the second inning, Yaz hit a home run off Guidry. Boston was up 2-0 in the seventh when Bucky Dent came up with two on and two out. The Yankees shortstop had only 16 extra-base hits on the season. Dent broke his bat on Torrez's second pitch and fouled the ball off his instep; he continued only after having it numbed with ethyl chloride. Dent swung at the next pitch and poked a harmless-looking fly that somehow carried into the screen atop Fenway's Green Monster to give New York a 3-2 lead.

That's where the highlight films end, but the game went on. In the eighth, Jackson hit a two-run shot. It turned out to be the margin of victory as the Red Sox scored twice off a shaky Gossage in the bottom of the inning. Down 5-4 in the bottom of the ninth with one out and Rick Burleson on first, Jerry Remy hit a liner to right that Lou Piniella lost in the sun. The quick-thinking Piniella acted as though he had it, and by sheer luck, the ball came right to him on a bounce. Piniella's decoy prevented Burleson from going to third, where he would have scored when Jim Rice hit a fly for the second out. Instead, Boston's season ended when Yastrzemski popped up to third baseman Graig Nettles.

Bucky Dent, who hit a three-run homer to give New York the lead, was an unlikely hero of the 1978 division playoff game. He averaged less than one homer per every 100 at-bats during his career. Boston pitcher Mike Torrez said that the extra time that Dent took after he hit a foul ball off of his foot robbed Torrez of some concentration.

Ron Guidry goes 25-3

Ron Guidry's 1978 season ranks as one of the greatest pitching seasons ever. With 25 wins in 28 decisions, Guidry compiled an .893 winning percentage; only Johnny Allen's 15-1 1937 campaign and reliever Elroy Face's 18-1 season in 1959 were better. Guidry led the American League in ERA at 1.74 and fewest hits per game at 6.1; he kept opponents to a minuscule .193 batting average. His nine shutouts were the most by an AL lefthander since Babe Ruth also threw nine shutouts in 1916.

Guidry went 2-0 in postseason play as the Yankees won their second straight World Championship and was the runaway winner in the Cy Young voting. But in spite of turning in a near-perfect performance that seemed to be the very definition of "most valuable," Guidry was narrowly defeated by Boston's Jim Rice in a controversial MVP vote.

PIRATES COME BACK TO WIN WORLD SERIES

Willie Stargell

The 1979 World Series was a rematch of the 1971 Series between the Pittsburgh Pirates and the Baltimore Orioles. The Orioles were seeking to avenge the defeat they suffered after being up in that Series 2-0. This time, however, they would have to do it against "The Family," led by team father-figure, co-NL MVP Award-winner (with Keith Hernandez), and inspirational leader Willie "Pops" Stargell. The disco dance craze was at its zenith in 1979, and one of the top hits that summer was "We Are Family" by Sister Sledge. The Pirates adopted the song as their theme.

The Pirates danced over the favored Cincinnati Reds in the National League Championship Series, beating them in three straight games on the strength of Stargell's MVP performance. The 38-year-old captain won game one with a three-run 11th-inning homer, hit a single and a double in the Pirates' 10-inning game two victory, and belted a homer and a double in the 7-1 game three triumph.

The slogan-less Orioles, on the other hand, stuck to the business of baseball, concentrating on giving solid pitching performances and racking up home runs. In the first game of the World Series, lefty Mike Flanagan made five first-inning runs—highlighted by a two-run homer from Doug DeCinces—stand up in a 5-4 victory. Although Pittsburgh won game two, the Orioles thumped the Bucs in a pair of scoring outbursts, 8-4 and 9-6 (winning the latter game after being down 6-3).

Stargell had gone 5-for-9 in the last two games, but despite wasting Pops's effort the Pirates refused to think negatively. In game five, the Pirates bombarded Baltimore for seven runs in the last three innings. The Orioles were confident going into game six, however. They were returning home and they had the great veteran righty Jim Palmer. Although Palmer pitched well, John Candelaria and Kent Tekulve were better, combining for a seven-hit shutout in a 4-0 Pittsburgh victory.

Baltimore jumped out to an early 1-0 lead in game seven; Stargell, however, wasn't about to see his family denied. The man who gave out "Stargell Stars" to his teammates during the season for making big plays deserved one of his own in the sixth after he belted a two-run homer off Scott McGregor, his third of the Series. Meanwhile, Pirates relievers Don Robinson, Grant Jackson, and Tekulve stifled the Orioles, as the Pittsburgh offense (which batted .323 for the seven games) tacked on two more runs in the ninth to take the crown.

Stargell finished the seven games with a .400 batting average, an .833 slugging average, three homers, seven runs scored, and seven RBI. This offensive output earned him the Series MVP Award. In the Steel City that evening, they were dancing in the streets.

Willie "Pops" Stargell on his way to first. In retrospect, his 1979 stats might make it seem he was a sentimental choice for the NL MVP Award, but there is no way to measure inspirational influence. In ten postseason games in 1979, he hit .415, clubbed five homers, had 13 RBI, and scored nine runs.

Willie "Pops" Stargell

Until his MVP season in 1979, Willie Stargell was one of baseball's best-kept secrets. Stargell became the leader for the Pittsburgh Pirates when the great Roberto Clemente died tragically after the 1972 season.

Although he led the NL in 1973 with 44 homers and 119 RBI, Willie lost the MVP Award to Pete Rose (he also lost in 1971 despite a league-leading 48 homers). "Pops" improved with age, carrying Pittsburgh to a pennant, and batting .281 with 32 homers and 82 RBI at the age of 38 to share the MVP with Keith Hernandez. The NLCS MVP, Stargell batted .400 in the seven-game World Series victory over the Baltimore Orioles to capture a sweep of MVP awards.

Steve Carlton

PHILLIES WIN THEIR FIRST WORLD CHAMPIONSHIP

As the 1980 decade broke open, there remained one of the 16 major league teams from 1901 that had yet to win a World Series. The closest the Philadelphia Phillies had come to the crown in their 97-year history was in 1915 and 1950, when they won pennants, and in 1964, when they lost the pennant in the last week of the season.

Now, however, the Phillies were a National League power, having played in (and lost) the Championship Series in 1976, 1977, and 1978. They hoped this year's race to the NL East pennant (they beat Montreal by a game) would carry them to a title. Their opponent would be the pitching-plentiful Houston Astros.

Houston gave Philadelphia's Pete Rose, Mike Schmidt, Tug McGraw & Co. all they could handle. After the Phillies won game one, Houston pulled out two extra-inning games, the second one on a combined 11-inning shutout by Joe Niekro and Dave Smith. The Astros had the Phillies on the brink of defeat in game four, leading 2-0 going into the eighth, but Philadelphia fought back to make it 3-2. Houston tied it in the bottom of the ninth, but the Phillies won the third straight extra-inning game of the NLCS with two runs in the 10th.

One of the most exciting Championship Series ever gained more intensity in game five. The lead changed hands four times until, after nine innings, it was seven-all. The Phillies squeezed across a run in the 10th for the win.

A successor to the NLCS, the World Series seemed almost anticlimactic. The Phillies kept up their momentum, however, winning the first two games in Philadelphia after being down 4-0 (to win 7-6) and 4-2 (to win 6-4). Kansas City bounced back in its home park, taking the next two games 4-3 (in 10 innings) and 5-3.

In the pivotal fifth game, Kansas City led 3-2 after six innings and the Phillies brought in McGraw, the veteran reliever. While he kept the Royals at bay, his teammates scored two runs in the ninth to go ahead 4-3. McGraw, who always had a flair for the dramatic, gave Phillies fans a scare when he walked the bases loaded in the bottom of the ninth before finally saving the game.

In game six, Phillies ace lefthander Steve Carlton held the Royals to one run for seven innings, while Philadelphia scored four. In came McGraw again, walking the bases loaded three times in the last two innings. Each time, however, he managed to get the big out, including a foul pop-up that bounced out of catcher Bob Boone's mitt and into Pete Rose's glove.

When Willie Wilson of the Royals struck out for a record 12th time to end the game, the City of Brotherly Love boasted a World Champion.

Mike Schmidt takes one deep in the 1980 Series. His homer in game three was his first in 19 postseason contests. He got his second homer in game five. Schmidt was named the fall classic Most Valuable Player for driving in seven runs while hitting .381 and slugging .714.

George Brett ends season with a .390 average

When George Brett won his first AL batting title in 1976 by hitting .333, it seemed a matter of time before the Kansas City third baseman would flirt with the .400 mark.

Playing through nagging injuries in 1980, he was hitting .337 by the All-Star break. His average steadily rose throughout the summer. On August 17, he went 4-for-4 to reach the magic .400 figure. With a bit more than two weeks left in the season, Brett first slumped then rallied in the season's final days, going 10-for-19. He closed the season hitting .390 (the highest average since 1941). He also had 24 homers, 118 RBI, and a league-best .664 slugging average, all of which earned him the AL MVP Award.

RICKEY HENDERSON SWIPES 130 BASES

There was a time when stolen base records could be neatly divided into pre-Maury Wills and post-Maury Wills records. Before Wills, the NL record-holder for stolen bases in a season was Cincinnati's Bob Bescher, who swiped 81 in 1911. Bescher was still the NL leader 51 years later when Wills stole 104. It was the same story in the AL, where the pre-Wills major league record of 96 was set by Ty Cobb in 1915. New major league marks were set in 1974 by Lou Brock and in 1982 by Rickey Henderson. The list of 100-stolen base seasons grew to Wills, Brock, Henderson, and Vince Coleman.

Henderson's career as a basestealer began when Billy Martin introduced "Billy Ball" in order to stimulate a powerless Oakland offense. As Martin put it: "I managed around him. If Rickey got on base, we scored runs." Henderson's stolen base total jumped from 33 to 100 in 1980, and the A's moved from last place to second. Billy Ball took the A's to the strike-year playoffs in 1981, but they lapsed to 94 losses in 1982.

It was the lost 1982 season that enabled Martin to turn Henderson completely loose on the base paths. With the team going nowhere, he stole second and third with abandon, regardless of game situations. Although his success rate fell to 75 percent (excellent, but more than five points below his career percentage) and he set a new major league record with 42 times caught stealing, Henderson's 130 steals smashed Brock's major league record by a dozen.

Henderson stole his 100th base early in August. When he went against Brewer pitcher Mike Caldwell on August 26, Henderson had 117 steals (and Brock was in attendance). He opened the game with a single. Caldwell attempted to keep Henderson close to the bag, but on the fourth pitch he took off and was safe at second, tying Brock's record. Henderson was unable to break Brock's record the rest of the game. The next night off of Doc Medich, Henderson walked his first time up. After Medich threw several times to first to lessen Henderson's lead at first, the pitcher brought the pitch home. Henderson flew toward second and got his 119th steal. The game was stopped for a short ceremony. When the contest continued, the new record-holder went on to steal three more bases.

What really sets Henderson apart is that basestealing is not the strongest part of his game. The main thing he does is score runs—around 100 a year. He also delivers about a .290 batting average, a .400 on-base average, and power (he holds the major league record for most career home runs leading off a game). Henderson is one of the top leadoff men in the game's history.

Top: *Rickey Henderson picks on the pennant-winning Brewers for his record 119th steal in 1982. An accomplished base thief and hitter from day one of his pro career* (bottom), *Henderson nevertheless spent three and one-half years in the minors, mainly in an effort to hone his fielding skills.*

One of the era's elite, Rickey Henderson has come to be regarded as the model leadoff hitter.

Rickey Henderson will likely be the first lefty-throwing and righthanded hitter (besides pitchers) to make the Hall of Fame (this page). Henderson poses with Lou Brock the night that he broke Brock's record (opposite page). In 1982, Henderson also set a major league record when he was nabbed 42 times.

NOLAN RYAN BEATS STEVE CARLTON TO STRIKEOUT RECORD

Nolan Ryan

Walter Johnson's all-time record of 3,508 career strikeouts was once considered as unbreakable as Babe Ruth's 714 home runs. Once Hank Aaron busted Ruth's mark, however, no career record seemed safe. By the start of the 1980s, six hurlers—Gaylord Perry, Nolan Ryan, Tom Seaver, Steve Carlton, Don Sutton, and Phil Niekro—had reached or were gaining on 3,000 lifetime Ks.

By 1983, Ryan and Carlton were not only in a position to pass Johnson easily, they were on track to post more than 4,000 lifetime strikeouts. The only question was: Who would break Johnson's record first?

It was fitting that the man who threw a fastball nicknamed "Ryan's Express" would be the one to overtake a pitcher nicknamed "Big Train." Ryan started the 1983 season 60 Ks ahead of Carlton (3,494 to 3,434). Ryan needed just five strikeouts to break Johnson's record when he started against the Montreal Expos on April 27. Without his usually explosive fastball, it took Ryan until the eighth inning to make history. He struck out Brad Mills looking at a curveball for the 3,509th.

Almost a month later, Carlton got his 3,509th K when he struck out San Diego's Garry Templeton. The race was on for Carlton to catch Ryan for the career lead. Ryan injured his thigh in early May and missed a month. On June 7, Carlton topped Ryan with 3,522 strikeouts. That night, Ryan fanned three to remain in second place, but in his next start, he whiffed 12—and the two artists were tied at 3,535.

Baseball fans were excited at the prospect of watching this duel all summer long. Carlton, however, pulled away in August and ultimately led the league with 277 Ks (Ryan had 183). That June, *The New York Times* had said, "Despite his being two years older than Ryan at 38, Carlton is likely to be around longer." In October, *The Sporting News* wrote, "With over 3,700 strikeouts, Carlton's record is as out of reach as DiMaggio's 56-game hitting streak or Hack Wilson's 190 RBI."

How wrong those venerable papers of record were. Ryan went ahead of Carlton by two at the end of 1984 and pulled away in '85, ultimately reaching the amazing total of 5,000 strikeouts in 1989.

Carlton retired after the 1987 season with 4,652 lifetime strikeouts and is still second behind Ryan on the all-time list. Gaylord Perry also passed Johnson by the end of 1983.

The New York Times assessed Ryan's lifetime achievement by saying that if a player had passed Ruth's homer record by the same percentage that Ryan was ahead of Johnson, he would have 980 homers. Ryan's response was "guess I'm going for 1,000 homers."

Top: *Nolan Ryan throwing the pitch to become the all-time strikeout king. Also the all-time walk king, Ryan topped Early Wynn's career record of 1,775 in 1981 without fanfare. Steve Carlton (bottom), usually deaf throughout his career to both criticism and cheers, here acknowledges the tribute paid him by fans when he catches Walter Johnson.*

DWIGHT GOODEN SHATTERS HERB SCORE'S ROOKIE STRIKEOUT RECORD

When he showed up in his first major league training camp in 1984, Dwight Gooden was 19 years old. The leading pick for the New York Mets in the 1982 draft, Gooden dominated Class-A ball his second year in the minors, going 19-4 with a phenomenal 300 strikeouts in 191 innings. The front office debated the issue of Gooden, and whether or not he should get more seasoning on the farm. Newly named Mets manager Davey Johnson, who held that the righthander was ready for the majors, won the argument, and Gooden proved him right.

With a fastball that exploded as it reached the strike zone and a curveball that broke so sharply it was called "Lord Charles" (other hurlers' curves are called simply "Uncle Charlie"), Gooden was one of the greatest pitching phenomenons in history. He was a prime factor in the first winning season for the Mets since 1976.

Gooden made his debut on April 7, pitching five innings in a 3-2 win over Houston. He carried a no-hitter into the eighth inning against Pittsburgh two months later, finally winning 2-1. He was the youngest player ever selected to the All-Star Game in July and in the first of his two shutout innings, he struck out the side.

As the season reached into September, an avalanche of rookie strikeout records fell. On August 27, Gooden broke Gary Nolan's record for Ks by a teenage rookie (206). During a one-hitter against the Chicago Cubs on September 7, Gooden's 11 Ks shattered Grover Alexander's NL rookie record of 227 strikeouts. In his next start, Gooden struck out 16 Pirates to break Herb Score's rookie record of 245 Ks set in 1955.

Gooden followed that pitching performance with another 16 strikeouts against Philadelphia, setting an NL record for Ks in two consecutive games with 32 (shattering the record held by the great Sandy Koufax) and a modern major league record of 43 Ks in three consecutive games. As Gooden's legend grew, Shea Stadium fans started hanging "Ks" signs for each strikeout that Doc notched.

Overall, Gooden went 17-9, was second in the league in ERA with a 2.60 mark, and set the rookie strikeout record with an astounding 276 Ks. He also established a major league record with an average of 11.39 strikeouts per nine innings and led the league in allowing the fewest hits per game, 6.65. In the Rookie of the Year election, Gooden received 23 out of a possible 24 first-place votes, becoming the youngest player to win the award.

A pitcher this young would seem highly susceptible to the sophomore jinx, but Gooden struck out the hex as well. He was even better in the 1985 season, winning the NL triple crown of pitching (wins, ERA, and strikeouts) and the Cy Young Award.

Dwight Gooden's rookie showing was hardly a surprise to 1983 Carolina League batters, who were fanned 300 times by him in only 191 innings. No teenage pitcher in this century has approached the kind of all-around year that Gooden had. To find a parallel, one must go back to 1887 when Silver King, also just age 19, won 37 games for the St. Louis Browns.

PETE ROSE SLAMS HIS 4,192ND HIT TO BEST TY COBB

When 22-year-old Pete Rose showed up at the Cincinnati Reds training camp in 1963, few of the team's veterans thought he had a chance to make the cut. His skills seemed average at best. He did, however, have a strong point—hustling. During his career, he developed another specialty—accumulating base hits.

Two years after winning the NL Rookie of the Year Award, the switch-hitting Rose led the league in hits with 209. He had 1,000 hits at the midway point of 1968, and just five years later he was up to 2,000. "My goal," he had said in 1972, "is 3,000. If I can play 150 games for the next five years, I'll reach 3,000 on July 16, 1977 . . . no, make that 1978."

Rose was as clairvoyant as he was cocky. On May 5, 1978, he became only the 13th man to pass the 3,000 hit mark; he had also tied the NL record for hits in 44 consecutive games. And Rose, just 36 years old, was showing no signs of letting up.

Not only did it appear possible that Rose could get 4,000 hits, it also seemed that Ty Cobb's all-time record of 4,191 hits might be in jeopardy.

After the 1978 season, Rose signed as a free agent with the Philadelphia Phillies and promptly had his 10th 200-hit season, a record. He led the Phillies to the World Series in 1980, and his 185 hits put him at the 3,547 mark, fourth all-time behind Stan Musial, Hank Aaron, and Ty Cobb.

The years looked as if they were catching up with Rose when in 1983, at age 42, he knocked only 121 hits. Just 201 hits away from the record going into '84, he signed with the Montreal Expos, then returned later in the season to his hometown Reds as player/manager. Rose was only 94 hits behind Cobb by year's end, and the nationwide countdown was on.

Playing as the Reds part-time first baseman in 1985, Rose posted 90 hits by the weekend of September 6. The Reds were in Chicago and, as manager, Rose could have kept himself out of the lineup to ensure breaking the record in Cincinnati. He felt he needed to play for the team to win, however, and he went on to tie Cobb at 4,191 hits on Sunday, September 8.

Three days later, 47,237 fans packed Riverfront Stadium (only a few miles from where Rose grew up) to witness history. In the first inning, Rose faced San Diego Padres righthander Eric Show. With the count 2-1, Show threw a slider inside. Rose fought the pitch off and drove it to left-center field for a single. The game was halted. As the crowd gave Rose a standing ovation, his son ran out to first base. The all-time base hits leader, never one to show any emotion on a baseball field other than grit and hustle, hugged his son and cried.

Top: *Pete Rose singles off of Eric Show, getting his 4,192nd base hit, more than any other player in baseball history.* Bottom: *A spectator's view of Rose singling in Riverfront Stadium on September 11, 1985, to break Ty Cobb's record.*

This page: *Padres first baseman Steve Garvey smiles as Pete Rose shows the crowd his new ranking on the all-time career base hits list. Opposite page: Rose as a rookie second baseman in 1963. During his career, Rose put in at least one full season as a regular at five different positions, a modern major league record.*

**Pete Rose was consistent: He had
10 seasons with 200-plus hits and
18 years with 150-plus safeties.**

ROYALS RALLY FROM A 3-1 GAME DEFICIT IN BOTH ALCS AND SERIES

George Brett

The Kansas City Royals were one of the best teams in the major leagues during the first half of the 1980 decade, yet they had just a single AL pennant (in 1980) and one AL West title (in 1984) to show for it. In 1985, however, the Royals produced two of the greatest postseason come-from-behind victories ever.

Led by superstar George Brett and Cy Young Award-winner Bret Saberhagen, the Royals went all the way to the ALCS only to fall behind the Toronto Blue Jays three games to one in the best-of-seven series. Setting in motion a recovery, Danny Jackson hurled a shutout for a 2-0 Royal victory in game five. On to the fifth inning of game six, where Brett (who had gone 4-for-4 in Kansas City's crucial third-game victory) whaled a homer to untie the two-all score and take the win.

Game seven was no contest. The bullpen (minus Saberhagen, who was knocked out of the game by a line drive off his pitching hand) held down the Jays while the Royals exploded for four runs in the sixth on the way to a 6-2 victory.

Pitted against their Missouri state cousins, the St. Louis Cardinals, the Royals lost games one and two of the "I-70" Series in Kansas City. Not only had just seven teams rebounded from such a deficit, no team had ever done it after blowing the first two in its home park. The Royals, however, were old hands at the business of comebacks.

After Saberhagen lifted the Royals out of impending doom by pitching a six-hitter for a 6-1 game three victory, John Tudor of the Cards returned them to the brink of defeat with a shutout. The Royals answered with a five-hitter, 6-1 game five victory from Danny Jackson.

Back in Kansas City, Danny Cox of the Cardinals and Charlie Leibrandt of the Royals hooked up in a scoreless seven-inning duel. St. Louis pushed across a run in the eighth and placed ace reliever Todd Worrell on the mound in the ninth. Jorge Orta led off with a grounder to first and, on a controversial call, was declared safe because Worrell pulled his foot off the bag. Replays showed that Orta was out.

After Jim Sundberg bunted into a force at third, a passed ball and a walk loaded the bases. Pinch hitter Dane Iorg then delivered a two-run, game-winning single.

Game seven was the Brett & Bret show, as the ALCS MVP Brett went 4-for-5 and the World Series MVP Saberhagen shut out the Cardinals on five hits in an 11-0 blowout. Kansas City had finally won its first World Championship, and no team had ever fought as hard for the victory.

Danny Jackson keyed the 1985 Kansas City championship run. He tossed two complete-game wins in both game fives of the ALCS and the fall classic. The 1985 Royals were the first AL expansion team to win a World Championship. Their manager, Dick Howser, had been a star rookie shortstop 24 years earlier for the Kansas City Athletics.

BILL BUCKNER'S BOOT REKINDLES METS IN WORLD SERIES

Gary Carter

Eleven years after the Boston Red Sox had been in one of the most memorable sixth games of the World Series, they found themselves in another one. Unlike 1975, when the Red Sox triumphed over the Reds on a Carlton Fisk home run, Boston came up on the short end this time, and largely because of an easily playable ground ball.

The New York Mets, who had won 108 games during the regular season and took the NL East by 21½ games, were favorites to win the championship. Boston was 95-66 on the season. Both teams won closely contested League Championship Series.

The Mets dropped their first two home games against Boston 1-0 and 9-3. The New York bats did wake up in Fenway Park, where they won the first two games 7-1 and 6-2. Bruce Hurst, who had shut out the Mets in game one, then pitched a 4-2 contest, putting the BoSox one game from an upset Series title.

Tied three-all after nine innings, game six appeared in the bag for Beantown when Sox outfielder Dave Henderson homered to lead off the 10th. Then a Wade Boggs double and a Marty Barrett single gave Boston what seemed to be an important insurance run. As Mets Wally Backman and Keith Hernandez went down against Red Sox reliever Calvin Schiraldi, fans prepared to celebrate their first Series title since 1918, when Babe Ruth pitched for Boston.

Gary Carter kept the Mets alive with a single to center. Then Kevin Mitchell, batting for reliever Rick Aguilera, knocked a single to center. Although Schiraldi got two strikes on Ray Knight, the third baseman fought off a fastball and blooped a single to center, driving in one run and putting the tying one on third.

Bob Stanley relieved Schiraldi and faced Mookie Wilson. With the count 2-2, Wilson fouled off three pitches. Stanley's next delivery, low and inside, hit off catcher Rich Gedman's glove; Mitchell danced down the line with the run that tied it. With Knight now in scoring position, Wilson hit two more pitches foul. "I just wasn't going to strike out in that spot," he said. Wilson tapped Stanley's next pitch down the first-base line for an apparent third out. As Boston first baseman Bill Buckner bent down to field the ball, however, it skipped through his legs. Knight brought home the winning run.

The Red Sox went up in game seven 3-0 before the Mets exploded with eight runs between the sixth and eighth innings. The New York team went on to win the game 8-5. Another championship had slipped beyond Boston's—and Billy Buckner's—grasp.

Jesse Orosco picked up two saves in the World Series, pitching five and two-thirds scoreless innings. He also picked up three wins in the NLCS. Here he leaps for joy after striking out Kevin Bass to beat the Astros in game six after 16 innings 7-6.

Dave Henderson

Henderson's blast wins game five of ALCS

The American League Championship Series in 1986 produced one of the most exciting games in postseason play. The Boston Red Sox were trailing the 1986 ALCS to the California Angels three games to one, losing game five 5-2, and down to their last inning. Don Baylor hit a two-run homer, cutting the deficit to one with one out. Angels manager Gene Mauch brought in lefty Gary Lucas after the second out; Lucas hit the next batter with a pitch.

In came California's ace righty reliever Donnie Moore to face Dave Henderson. With two strikes on him, Henderson belted a homer for the Boston lead. The BoSox took the game in the 11th inning. They carried the momentum to Boston, where they beat the Angels 10-4 and 8-1 for the pennant.

Bill Buckner (this page) *after he flubbed Mookie Wilson's easy grounder to keep the Mets alive in game six of the 1986 World Series. Mookie Wilson* (opposite page, top) *taps Bob Stanley's pitch down the first base side toward Buckner. Wilson's knubber scored Ray Knight to win game six for the Mets. Dwight Gooden* (opposite page, bottom) *went 17-6 in the regular season and had a 1.06 ERA in the NLCS. In the fall classic, however, he lost two games and had an 8.00 ERA.*

Bill Buckner played 162 games at first base for Boston in 1985, notching a record 184 assists. He will be remembered, however, for one that got away.

MARK McGWIRE BLASTS ROOKIE-RECORD 49 HOMERS

The 1987 season was a bonanza year for offense in general and the home run in particular. The many hitting milestones from that year included a new major league record for total home runs with 4,458; 20 or more homers hit by a record 51 AL players; three teams (Detroit, Toronto, and Baltimore) hit over 200; Toronto hit a record 10 homers in one game.

Amid all this excitement and controversy, it's not hard to see how the Oakland Athletics Mark McGwire's total obliteration of the rookie home run record got somewhat lost in the shuffle. McGwire actually broke a number of rookie home run records, many of which had stood for a long time. Cleveland's Al Rosen set the AL mark in 1950 with 37. The NL record had been set by Wally Berger, who hit 38 in 1930, and matched by Frank Robinson in 1956.

Great things were not predicted for McGwire in 1987. In fact, he came into spring training as a long shot to unseat Carney Lansford at third; the A's plan was to give first base to Rob Nelson, who had swatted 52 home runs over the previous two minor league seasons. But McGwire looked so good in camp that he was given Nelson's job in spite of a .167 spring-training batting average. Teammate Jose Canseco predicted: "[McGwire is] going to hit 30 homers and drive in more than 100 runs."

McGwire made half a prophet out of Canseco by hitting 33 homers before the All-Star break. Inevitably, speculation started about the rookie's chances of breaking Roger Maris's home run record. Of course, there are reasons why many more than 100 men have hit 40-plus home runs in a season and only 17 have reached 50, and McGwire was much too level-headed to put that kind of pressure on himself. Things were tough enough already with American League pitchers being a little more careful with him in the second half; he hit only three home runs (with only 12 RBI) in August. He had the flu so severely during that time that he lost 10 pounds. McGwire, though, came back healthy, laid off bad pitches, and rebounded with a nine-homer September to break the rookie home run record with 49, a margin of almost 30 percent.

McGwire ended the season with the rookie-season records not only for home runs but for total bases with 344, for slugging percentage with .618, and for most extra bases in a season with 183. He tied the team RBI mark of 118. Against Cleveland in June, he hit five home runs in two games, and he scored nine runs in nine consecutive plate appearances, tying another AL record. For the season, 17 of McGwire's home runs came on first pitches, while 20 homers came when he was leading off the inning.

McGwire became the first unanimous Rookie of the Year selection since Carlton Fisk in 1972.

Few rookies have hit more homers during their first season in the majors than they did during their best year in the minors; Mark McGwire clubbed more dingers as a frosh than he had in his entire three-year minor league career.

OREL HERSHISER BREAKS DON DRYSDALE'S RECORD FOR SCORELESS INNINGS

I t is referred to as "a career year," that one amazing season when a baseball player puts it all together and plays better than anyone, including himself, ever deemed he could. Orel Leonard Hershiser IV had one of those career years in 1988, the season in which he shattered one of the game's most unbreakable of records—Don Drysdale's streak of 58 consecutive scoreless innings.

A long and lean 29-year-old Los Angeles Dodgers righthander, Hershiser had been one of the National League's best pitchers since coming up in 1984. Nicknamed "Bulldog" by Dodgers manager Tommy Lasorda, Hershiser featured an above-average fastball, an outstanding curve, a tremendous sinker—and the control to throw them anywhere in the strike zone. After four years in the league, he had become an intelligent hurler, studying hitters and pitching to their weaknesses.

Hershiser was in the midst of dissecting the NL's batters when the streak originated on August 30. Going 17-8 and pitching the Dodgers to the NL West pennant, he just then seemed to shift into high gear. One team after another fell under his shutout spell—Atlanta (3-0), Cincinnati (5-0), Atlanta (1-0), Houston (1-0), and San Francisco (3-0)—until September 28, when Hershiser was just nine shutout innings shy from tying the benchmark set by Don Drysdale, another great Dodgers righthander. Hershiser matched the 20-year-old record during that game, putting up nine goose eggs against the San Diego Padres. The Dodger offense, however, also failed to score, giving Hershiser a chance to pitch another inning and break the record. "It was the best I'd ever seen [Hershiser] pitch," said Padre Tony Gwynn, one of the game's best hitters. "I grounded out four times on a sinker and he set me up differently each time."

The only question that remained was whether or not the pitching sensation would last through a 10th inning. Lasorda and pitching coach Ron Perranowski persuaded Hershiser, who said he would be satisfied sharing the record with Drysdale, to go for the break. "If he hadn't," said Drysdale at a press conference after the game, "I would have gone out there and kicked him in the rear." Hershiser took the mound and retired the Padres in order, pitching 59 consecutive scoreless innings.

Hershiser extended his career year into postseason play, claiming both the NLCS and World Series MVP awards in leading the Dodgers to a World Championship. By opening the NLCS against the Mets with eight shutout innings, Hershiser racked up 67 straight innings in which he was not scored upon; he then closed the series with a shutout in game seven. He went on to keep the Oakland A's scoreless in one of the World Series games. The Cy Young Award-winner finished the season with a 23-8 record and a 2.26 ERA.

An ailing arm laid Orel Hershiser low in 1990 after he topped the NL in innings pitched the previous two seasons. Only Dave Parker, who rapped a trio of singles, stood between Hershiser and a no-hitter in his masterful three-hit 6-0 shutout of the A's in game two of the 1988 World Series.

KIRK GIBSON'S WORLD SERIES HOME RUN SPURS DODGERS

In the climatic scene of the film *The Natural,* damaged baseball player Roy Hobbs wins the championship by hitting a game-ending home run so prodigious it destroys a light tower. In game one of the 1988 World Series, life imitated art.

The Los Angeles Dodgers faced the Oakland Athletics by virtue of beating the New York Mets and Boston Red Sox, respectively. The A's—with sluggers Jose Canseco, Mark McGwire, and Dave Parker, and a fine pitching staff headed by Dave Stewart and baseball's best reliever Dennis Eckersley—had won 104 games during the regular season and were favored to beat the Dodgers and their pop-gun attack. The Dodgers, however, had two points in their favor: They possessed Cy Young Award-winner and NLCS Most Valuable Player Orel Hershiser and league MVP Kirk Gibson.

As the Series got underway, however, it appeared that Gibson's inspirational leadership would be coming more from the bench than the field. He had strained his left hamstring in game five of the playoffs and he hadn't swung at a pitch since injuring his right knee in game seven.

Los Angeles got power early from outfielder Mickey Hatcher, who homered in the bottom of the first. The A's answered back with Canseco's grand slam in the next inning. A Dodger run in the sixth made it 4-3. When the game reached the eighth inning, Gibson picked his body off the trainer's table, put an ice bag on his knee, suited up, took some practice swings off a batting tee, and told manager Tommy Lasorda he was able to hit if he was needed. Gibson hadn't even been able to swing a bat that morning.

Eckersley walked Mike Davis leading off the last of the ninth. Light-hitting Dave Anderson had been put on deck as a decoy. Gibson emerged from the dugout, hobbled to the plate, and looked completely overwhelmed as he fouled off two pitches. When he hit the next slider foul, he almost fell out of the batter's box. A few pitches later, Davis stole second. All Gibson needed to bring him home to tie the game was a base hit.

On a 3-2 count, Eckersley appeared to throw a slider down and away. Gibson, however, reached out with his powerful arms and got enough wrist action into the swing to, amazingly, send the ball far into right field and out of the park for a game-winning home run.

As Gibson limped slowly around the bases, his arm raised in the air, Hall of Fame broadcaster Jack Buck probably echoed the feelings of a nation when he said, "I don't believe what I just saw." Neither did the A's, who won only game three and lost the Series four games to one.

Kirk Gibson, winner of the 1988 NL MVP, takes his most renowned cut of the season. That he was voted the award-winner prior to his postseason heroics makes the selecting committee seem prescient, the more so in that his regular season stats were not particularly impressive.

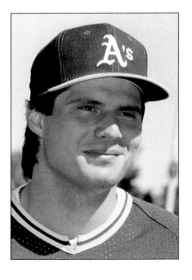

Jose Canseco's 40-40 season

Over the history of baseball, there have only been a handful of players—Willie Mays, Mickey Mantle, and Bobby Bonds—who could not only produce 30 to 50 homer seasons, but steal bases in bunches as well. None of them, however, did what the Oakland A's slugging outfielder accomplished in 1988. In the early part of the season, Jose Canseco predicted that he would slug 40 homers and steal 40 bases. At the time, he said that he was unaware that no one had ever done that before. Then, at the age of 24, the 230-pound Canseco went out and belted 42 home runs and stole exactly 40 bases. When he got his 40th swipe, he seemed relieved to have made his prediction come true. He didn't want to "end up short and say I stuck my foot in my mouth." The unanimous MVP Award-winner that year, he led the major leagues with 124 RBI 42 homers and a .569 slugging percentage.

Kirk Gibson finishes his swing (this page) *and leaps for joy when the ball clears the fence* (opposite page). *The Dodgers seemed to follow the example set by Gibson to beat the heavily favored Oakland A's in the fall classic, much the same way as they came out of nowhere to win the NL flag behind Gibson.*

Even Kirk Gibson admitted that it was a storybook finish. He limped to the plate to face baseball's best reliever. Looking overmatched against Dennis Eckersley, Gibson fouled off three pitches before parking a slider into the seats.

ROBIN YOUNT IS MVP
IN CENTER FIELD
AFTER WINNING AWARD
AT SHORTSTOP

Breaking into the Milwaukee lineup at shortstop in 1974, Robin Yount at age 18 became the youngest regular every-day player in history. In his first few seasons he hit around .250 with little power and had stretches when he struggled defensively; he led the AL in errors in 1975 with 44. Throughout the middle to late 1970s, nonetheless, Yount showed steady improvement in every phase of the game. In 1978, he led AL short-stops in double plays and total chances; in 1980, he led the league in dou-bles with 49 and hit .293 with 23 home runs.

Then came 1982, when Yount turned in one of the finest hitting sea-sons ever by a shortstop and won the AL MVP. He batted .331 with 46 dou-bles and 29 homers; he drove in 114 runs and scored 129 and carried the Brewers to the pennant. At .578, he led the league in slugging, something only three National League shortstops in this century—Ernie Banks, Arky Vaughan, and Honus Wagner—had ever accomplished; no AL shortstop had ever done it.

A 1984 shoulder injury forced Yount to make a detour to the outfield and put his status as a plausible future Hall of Famer in doubt. Yount's stats—an average of 32 doubles, seven triples, and 13 home runs over 11 seasons—stacked up well against the offensive production of many Hall of Fame shortstops, but they are nowhere near Cooperstown-quality for an outfielder.

Since then, at an age when most ballplayers are in decline, Yount slowly but surely put the pieces back together and returned to the form of 1980 to 1982. His arm came around, and he improved his defense enough that he was a better-than-average glove in center field. He batted over .300 every year since 1986 and had more than 190 hits from 1987 to '89.

Finally, in 1989, Yount proved that he had made it all the way back with his finest offensive season since the MVP year in 1982. He batted .318 and slugged .511, both post-1982 highs. He both scored and drove in 100 runs for the first time since '82 and played with incredible consistency: He hit over .300 every month except April and against both righthanders and lefties, and he hit .355 with runners in scoring position. Yount was "Mister Everything" for the light-hitting Brewers, leading the team in batting aver-age, slugging average, on-base average (.384), runs (101), RBI (103), hits (195), games (160), total bases (314), doubles (38), and triples (nine). He passed the 2,500-hit milestone in 1989 and even stole 19 bases. His value to his team was so obvious that Yount overcame Milwaukee's also-ran perfor-mance in the pennant race to win his second MVP Award.

Yount was considered to be the best player in his league in two differ-ent seasons at two of the most demanding positions in baseball—short-stop and center field—a feat that can be directly attributed to his out-standing work ethic.

In 1989, Robin Yount passed Gorman Thomas in home runs to give him the lead in every major Brewers' career hitting department except batting average and slugging percentage. Yount did not crack the .300 barrier until 1982, his ninth season. He then posted five straight .300-plus campaigns.

NOLAN RYAN PAINTS HIS SIXTH NO-HIT MASTERPIECE

As a member of the California Angels, Nolan Ryan threw four no-hitters in the three seasons between 1973 and 1975. His first was on May 15, 1973, against the Kansas City Royals. Two months later, he struck out 17 Detroit Tigers and walked four to record his second. On September 28, 1974, Ryan walked eight Minnesota Twins while striking out 15 for his third career no-hitter. He tied Sandy Koufax's career record of four by shutting down the Baltimore Orioles.

By 1981, however, Ryan still stood tied with Koufax for the record. Ryan had joined the Astros in 1980 after signing as a free agent. That year the 34-year-old righthander had one of his best seasons, going 11-5 with a league-leading 1.69 ERA. His fastball—"Ryan's Express"—still looked like a streak of lightning, his curveball still looked like it was falling off a table.

On September 26, Ryan broke the tie. Starting against the Los Angeles Dodgers at the Astrodome on national TV, Ryan struggled with his control the first three innings, walking three batters and throwing a wild pitch. "My back was hurting and I didn't have any rhythm in the early innings," Ryan said. Although he had 10 strikeouts over those first six innings, he let up in the final three to give him better control of his pitches. The strategy worked. Reggie Smith led off the ninth and Ryan threw three strikes by him. Ken Landreaux then grounded to first for the second out. On a 2-0 pitch, Ryan threw a big curve that Dusty Baker bounced to third base for an easy out. Ryan had his first no-hitter in six years and a new record.

In 1989, Ryan jumped to the Texas Rangers and led the AL that year with 301 strikeouts. On June 11, 1990, he was making his second start since coming off the 15-day disabled list with a stress fracture in his lower verte-brae. He was 4-3 at the time with a 5.11 ERA. The 43-year-old was facing the defending World Champion Oakland A's. "I was concerned with my back problems, and I said, 'Well, I'll just go seven innings,'" Ryan said later. "Then, I got through [the seventh inning], and I decided I'm not going to give in to it. Because I needed just six more outs."

The more than 30,000 Oakland fans chanted "Nolan! Nolan!" over the final innings. Ryan's son Reese sat on the bench with his pop, giving him encouragement. In the ninth inning, Ryan struck out leadoff batter Ken Phelps, got Rickey Henderson to ground out, and got Willie Randolph to foul out. When the final out was made, Ryan's Ranger teammates carried him off the field. Ryan struck out 14 and walked only two.

"It is certainly one of the special nights in my life," Ryan said.

Nolan Ryan pitching during his sixth no-hitter. Later in 1990, he won his 300th game, virtually assuring himself a place in the Hall of Fame. Unfortunately, earlier in his career some observers felt that he was only a one-pitch chucker who had a .500 record. Ryan has since silenced his critics.

Lynn Nolan Ryan being carried off the field by his teammates. While there have been several pitchers age 43 who have been effective in the majors, most have been knucklers or control pitchers. Ryan at age 43 is a strikeout king.